Inflation: The Silent Retirement Killer

DR. DAVID PHELPS, DDS

HOW TO OUTWIT THE FED AND THEIR **EXTRACTION OF YOUR WEALTH**

The Silent Retirement Killer

M E D I A
Rockwall, Texas

Inflation: The Silent Retirement Killer
How to Outwit the Fed and Their Extraction of Your Wealth

Copyright © 2022 Dr. David Phelps, DDS

All rights reserved. No part of this publication may be reproduced, stored in a retrieval system, or transmitted, in any form or by any means, electronic, mechanical, photocopying, recording, or otherwise, without the prior written permission of the copyright holder.

For information, address David Phelps International LLC,
519 E. IH 30 Suite 246, Rockwall, TX 75087

Cover Design by Monica Austin, Mocah Studio, LLC
Interior Design by Imagine!® Studios, www.ArtsImagine.com
Edited by Cheyne Minto

ISBN: 979-8-9860396-0-2 (hardback)
ISBN: 979-8-9860396-1-9 (paperback)

Library of Congress Control Number: 2022935981

First printing: April 2022

TABLE OF CONTENTS

Foreword . . . . *ix*

Introduction . . . . *xv*

CHAPTER ONE
A PRIMER ON MONEY & CONFISCATION 1

Money Is the Root of All Evil: When You Don't Control It 3
Tobacco as Currency 3
The Roman Empire 4
It's Not Worth a Continental 4
The United States of America 5
Creation of the Federal Reserve 6
Gold Confiscation by FDR 6
Cryptocurrency: Could History Repeat? 8
Bretton Woods Agreement 1944 9
The Death of the Gold Standard 11

CHAPTER TWO
INFLATION & HOW IT SHOWS UP IN OUR LIVES 13

Demand-Pull Inflation 14

    Cost-Push Inflation 15
    Rising Labor Costs Leads to Higher Inflation 17

CHAPTER THREE
MONETARY POLICY & TECHNIQUES OF THE FED ... 21

    Could the Fed Be Driving Us into an Inflationary Spiral? 22
    Market Operations and Quantitative Easing 23
    But Here's the Scary Part 25
    The Fed's Balance Sheet Has Exploded Since 2004! 26
    Modern Monetary Theory: Spending Doesn't Matter 27
    Reserve Requirements for Banks 29
    The Federal Funds Rate 30
    The Prime Lending Rate & Borrowing 33
    Why Isn't the Fed Addressing Inflation? 33

CHAPTER FOUR
IT'S BEGINNING TO LOOK A LOT LIKE THE '70s 35

    Government Spending on the War & The Great Society 36
    From LBJ to Nixon, Overspending Leads to Inflation 38
    Price Controls, Wage Freezes & the Death of the Gold Standard ... 39
    The Tax Burden Nearly Doubles! 41
    War and Oil Embargo 42
    Gas Lines, Energy Shortages, and Stock Market Collapse 44
    Update March 15th: Ukrainian War 45
    President Ford's Fight with Inflation: Pump & Tax 47
    Economic Migraine, Pain, and Bloody Stock Market 48
    Carter Gets Tough with Inflation: Take the Pain 49
    Carter Confronts the Nation and the Crisis of Confidence 51
    High-Interest Rates Squash Inflation and Kill the Economy
      (1979–1981) 53

The Reagan Revolution Begins 53
The Public Call for Volcker's Head!............................... 55
A Return to Normalcy!.. 55
*What Happened to Stock Market Returns During
    Inflationary Times?* 57

CHAPTER FIVE
INFLATION ROARS BACK TO LIFE 61

The Fed is Behind the Curve, and It Won't End Well 62
Curiosity, Evaluation, and Examination are Vital for Success 64
The Great Wealth Transfer....................................... 66
The Deficits Will Rise to Unsustainable Levels................... 68
Never Let a Crisis Go to Waste 71
Inflation Helps Pay Back Promises . . . With Inflated Dollars...... 73
Not Every Tax Bracket Is Indexed for Inflation 75
The 2018 Tax Cuts & Jobs Act Changed the CPI Index 75
Other Stealth Taxes 76
The Tax Bomb Waiting in IRA's 77
Losing Control Happens Quickly 79

CHAPTER SIX
STRATEGIES TO OFFSET THE EFFECTS OF
INFLATION IN YOUR FREEDOM PLAN 85

What to Do Now: 87
My Favorite Is Real Estate 99
A Word about Leverage... 101
Real Estate Is More Than Rental Properties 104
Do Your Due Diligence! 105
Take Action & Take Control of Your Future 106

CHAPTER SEVEN
LIVES TRANSFORMED BY SUSTAINABLE PASSIVE INCOME—THE FREEDOM FOUNDERS MODEL 109

Dr. Greg and Jackie Linney's Journey to Retirement Clarity & Certainty 110
Dr. Jim Rachor's Flight to Freedom and Time for Charity 111
Dr. Hiru and Sumit Mathur's Journey to Financial Freedom..... 112
Dr. Ben & Sondra Jensen from Darkness to Light............... 114
Could You Be Next? It's Possible! 115

About the Author... 117

Resources 121

Glossary 127

FOREWORD

Growing up, in a distant war-torn and third-world country in Africa, left indelible marks on my mind and philosophy. Adding to that, was the fact that I was raised by a family of multi-generational entrepreneurs. I have so many memories of those days and the deep, familial grooves that cut into my own preferences, instincts, habits, and ultimately, the life I live today. Of all the messages reflected to me by the successful businesses that my parents and extended family had built and run, the most valuable was that of dynamism. In a volatile third-world economy, the importance of staying dynamic as a business, in an extremely unpredictable economy, couldn't be overstated. It wasn't just because it was profitable, it was quite literally the only way to survive.

As a young boy, I clearly recall, every Friday, sitting in the Mazda pickup truck with Douglas. Douglas worked for one of my parents' businesses as a driver, shuttling people and things around town; he was also the general "Man Friday" tasked with taking care of anything that needed doing in and around the growing business. Each Friday, I would join him in the front of the company pickup for his three-times-weekly bank deposits. There on the front seat, nestled between us, was a small, fishing tackle-box. The contents of which represented the last 48 hours of cash generated at my parents' business. The total figure? Probably $5,000 in cash and almost the same again in checks. At the time, I was about 10 or 11-years-old and always enjoyed the conversations I had with Douglas, a wise and deeply loyal man who supported my parents and our family, as we supported him, for the length of his 32 years of employment. As soon as the ladies in the office had finished counting the cash, he would put it in this innocuous little box and drive off, without any sort of security, to Zimbank, our local bank trusted institution. I don't recall why I always found myself accompanying him on Fridays, but I always indulged in those conversations and the wisdom of one of the kindest men you'll ever meet.

Over the course of the next several years, the Zimbabwean economy experienced a period of hyperinflation that is now stuff for the record books. How it manifested for me and my family could fill a book of its own, but suffice to say this: that mere $5,000 cash deposit, repeated every Monday, Wednesday and Friday, became a million dollars in deposits, three times a week, just 15 years later. Now, of course, this innocuous little fishing box would no longer do it. In classic Zimbabwean fashion, my parents decided the solution was a steamer trunk. A large three-and-a-half foot by two-foot steel box with a lock on it, left in the back of the very same pickup truck and delivered, quite casually, three times a week. Now, this might suggest an enormous growth in business—watching deposits totaling $15,000 a week to becoming $3 million a week, 15 years later. After all, if I described those numbers to you in any other industry, you would assume that the ship of all ships had come in for my parents and family. The reality? Gross revenues over that time had fallen 84%.

Businesses were getting crushed. Inflation destroyed our currency and with it, the quality of life and the very fabric of our society. A business depositing $15,000 a week becoming $3 million a week would suggest an explosion of growth, but what it really reflected was life on the front lines of the fastest collapsing economy on earth. Among other business interests, my parents owned a gas and service station, and frequently experienced gas shortages that amounted to vehicles lined up 350 deep, stretching as far as two miles, in wait for their quota. Families would routinely wait as long as two weeks, lined up in their vehicles, inching forward a couple of hundred feet a day. Inevitably, conflicts would break out as some tried to jump the line or cut someone out, or the gas station would run dry before they made it to the pump and my parents would get the wrath of the angry mob.

Such is the nature of a society in decay, the chief cause of which is a protracted deterioration in the value and purchasing power of the nation's currency.

Throughout this journey of economic implosion in Zimbabwe, as both a child, a student, and ultimately an entrepreneur of my own, one of the most striking aspects of this deterioration was society's response to it. In every case where interest rates went from 15% to 18% or 20% to 30% on cash deposits, nobody was paying attention to the *larger trend*. Every rise in interest rates made those saving cash feel positive. I recall myself having a 22% savings account. Delighted with that sort of a return, I was blind to the trend itself. Any currency that can afford an interest payment of 22% is de facto imploding at a far greater rate in its relative strength. In every case where the cost of food or gasoline rose, (in many instances, grocery stores changing the prices throughout the day) business owners and consumers alike all seemed to treat these changes as *episodic*—just this particular interest rate increase or this particular week's shortage in bread, or gas, or fill in the blank.

In truth, the deterioration was systemic and structural and Zimbabwe was on a path to the complete financial and social destruction. The dynamism of entrepreneurship was the only thing that kept my family fed and supported the livelihood of its employees. Given the history of civil-war regime change, (three of which had occurred just in my parents' life, two in my own), dynamism of business was no different than the dynamism required for the general society just to survive. Change was the very nature of our lives. The only difference between the third-world economies and those of the Western world, such as the United

States, is the speed and size of those changes. What is a movement of the handle of the whip in the United States economy, is the tail end of that same whip in Zimbabwe. I'm so thankful for that brutal tuition, earned through the scar tissue of my parents and family and ultimately, myself as a business owner.

The critical piece of that lesson: dynamism and the ability to foresee and anticipate *change*.

For the last 40 years, the United States economy and its investors, citizens and entrepreneurs have enjoyed a period of near-perfect business conditions. Truly, the Goldilocks years—interest rates collapsing from 20% to 1%, equity markets booming, housing, stock and prices increasing almost unceasingly every year. And the biggest bond bull-market in world sovereign debt history. What a time it has been to be alive! How privileged we, here in the West, have been to navigate such calm waters with our businesses. How profitable and peaceful outside of the small random crisis or two it has been. Of all the frailties of the human intellect, one jumps out as the most dangerous: the reticular cortex, the pattern-seeking part of our ancient limbic-system. It's the part of the brain that helped us as more primitive hominids. Remember: red berry, dangerous; blue berry, safe.

The same part of the reticular cortex is what helps you see white pickup-trucks everywhere, once you've decided you want a white pickup-truck. What this part of the brain does in its pattern-seeking habits and instincts is to allow us to notice patterns which we immediately begin extrapolating into the future. That's all we do. The vast bulk of any economic or financial forecast you see, whether it's for a business or an economy at large, is simply that—an extrapolation of a trend that has already been going on for a long time. When the trend is large and strong and you're on the right side of it, this can be very profitable, very easy, and very predictable for business owners. That has been the case for the last 42 years here in the United States. The problem with this linear-extrapolation instinct that we have is that it fails us when it matters most: critical times of *change*. The system deep inside our very own brains undermines our ability to anticipate transitions and imagine or prepare for a future that no longer looks like the past we have lived through.

It is here that we need to dial back our aperture to a wider scope and truly understand not just our lived history, but the full sweeping narrative of the history that came long before us, including those of foreign cultures. Sadly, in the United States, this is something we don't do enough of. So here we sit toward the tail end of the Goldilocks era of business, entrepreneurship and investing in the United States. It is my conviction and clearly David's, through the pages of this book that the next 25 and 40 years will not necessarily look anything like those which got us to now. It is at this point that a whole new level of intellectual dynamism will be required. That dynamism must be rooted in a very clear grasp of the history of everything that brought us to where we are today.

That is the gift of David's message and the powerful treatise you hold in your hands.

Over the course of the pages that lie ahead, you are going to get an immaculate breakdown of every single critical episode of American financial, economic, monetary, and political individual issues that, with the full scope of this book, will show you the broader theme. As the old saying goes: history may not repeat, but it certainly rhymes. As David walks us through all the components of America's fiscal history, you will start to see trends emerge that will fit into your most recent experience. The case is a compelling one and very difficult to argue with. We've watched interest rates fall from 1981 until July of 2020 and seen commodity prices fall right alongside them.

The evidence suggests that that Goldilocks boom-era, of cheaper money, cheaper goods, a stable currency and rising asset prices appears to be coming to a close.

As David lays out so clearly over these pages and chapters ahead, this suggests that we are now entering a period where the exact opposite outcome is now the highest probability outcome. Rising interest rates, rising costs of goods and the structural damage this combination does to supply chains, businesses, households, profit margins and society at large. Most critically, the inevitable structural damage to the value of the currency itself. Essentially, what has worked up until now is unlikely to work as reliably, as predictably, or as profitably going forward. And it is this level of intellectual and financial dynamism that David's work is beautifully calling us to prepare for.

There are many reasons to admire David, not just for his own personal success, not just for his integrity, honesty, and authenticity, but also for his wisdom—born as those of others I admire, from the scar tissue of his own lived experience. You are going to read valuable words from one of my favorite people. He's one of my favorite people because he is somebody who eats his own cooking. The advisory, consulting, mentor, coaching world of today is laden with individuals that are experts on other people's ideas and experiences. What David shares and walks you through in these pages ahead is his own lived experience.

He is, truly a full-cycle entrepreneur.

There is not an environment that he hasn't navigated, a situation where he hasn't paid a price for being wrong, and personally profited from being right.

This book is a compilation, consolidation and distillation of all the greatest lessons that he has to share with us, as he does so profitably, so consistently and so powerfully for those wise enough to align themself with him as clients. To spend time with David is to spend time with those mentors I had as a young lad in one of the most dynamic and entrepreneurial environments that you could imagine. You are in good, wise and powerful hands.

Inflation is upon us. What worked up until now, is unlikely to serve us going forward.

The time for dynamism is now, and David is just the man to lead us.

Alastair J. Macdonald

INTRODUCTION

> *"Invest in inflation. It's the only thing going up."*
> **WILL ROGERS**

> *"Inflation is as violent as a mugger, as frightening as an armed robber and as deadly as a hitman."*
> **PRESIDENT RONALD REAGAN**

I purchased my first investment property in 1980. The mortgage financing on this property was 13.5%, and inflation was running at 14.5%. The property cash-flowed (produced income beyond the operating expenses and debt service) and created a capital gain profit of just over $50,000 over the four years I held and managed the property.

At that time, I didn't have any basis for determining if the market economics in 1980 were optimum or not for beginning my investment in real estate. Inflation ran over 7% for the decade from 1970 to 1980. I had no idea what the "right" interest rate should be in 1980. Instead, I did the math, purchased the property, and installed a renter for the next four years.

Over the next decade, inflation was moderated by the actions of Paul Volcker, Federal Reserve Chairman under Presidents Carter and Reagan, and interest rates began a multi-decade decline. Even though most of the investment properties I purchased during the '80s were financed at rates between 8.0% and 9.5%, I still earned money (cash flow) and made profits from those properties.

What about today? We're at a 40-year low for interest rates (now likely on the way up) as the first signs of inflation have begun to rear their ugly heads. Once inflationary trends take hold, it is very difficult to turn back. Inflation goes from an "event" to a "state." People's emotions and expectations take over and drive an inflationary sentiment that is very difficult to curtail. (The actions of Paul Volcker in 1980 caused a severe national recession before inflation was brought "under control.")

Since the massive pumping of Quantitative Easing (QE) and artificial lowering of interest rates by the Federal Reserve in the years following the Great Financial Recession (2008), economists have warned that inflation would eventually manifest. With inflation reaching levels today not seen since the early '80s, it's safe to say the tsunami of inflation is upon us.

But here's a warning: Do not be fooled by the early inflation numbers or buy into groupthink, believing this inflationary trend will end. I expect the numbers to subside later this year, and it will 'appear' as if inflation is declining. I warn you, however, it has only begun.

Throughout this book, I'll show you who profits and who is destroyed by inflation. I'll teach you how to navigate the storm and secure your wealth. I'll also show you how, in good times or bad, to safely build your wealth through alternative investments in real estate.

At the time of this book's publishing, the government CPI (Consumer Price Index) year-over-year inflation rate hit a 40-year high of 7.9% in March 2022. Realize that these are government-issued numbers and are highly manipulated.

As you'll learn, the Consumer Price Index (CPI) has been altered many times by the government. Created to track and measure the costs of goods and services purchased for consumption, the CPI can be envisioned as a shopping cart or basket full of goods and services you might purchase throughout the year—food, fuel, housing, medical services, education, recreation, etc. This CPI basket is tracked to determine how quickly prices are rising. The problem is, the true rate of inflation can be masked or altered if the basket of goods and services are changed, which is exactly what the government has done.

Using the old CPI basket from 1980, inflation would be over 15%! That would rank as the highest level of inflation since 1946. (More on government statistics and why it benefits them in the chapters to come).

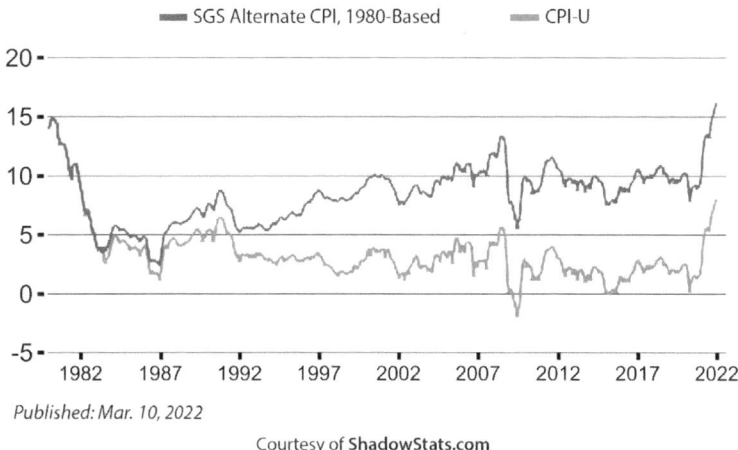

What Does This Mean for You and Your Family?

Every day I speak with professional practice owners and executives worried about outliving their income and the disastrous effects of inflation on their future. Some are burned out, bouncing from chair to chair, and dealing with insurance companies and staffing issues. Many are held captive by the faulty premise of Wall Street.

You know the spiel Wall Street tells us.

Accumulate money in tax-deferred investments until you reach a certain age, then slowly pull out 4–6% a year. But don't live to "age 95" and pray the stock market doesn't take a hit in the first few years of retirement. If it does, you're screwed!

With inflation eating away at returns and purchasing power, the dynamics and challenges have become exacerbated. Rising interest rates and inflation will slaughter fixed income investments, while the stock market will experience upheaval as rates rise and recession eventually washes upon our shores. Sadly, many investors have been forced into a precarious position, chasing yields and returns without knowing the risks that lie ahead.

If that sounds like it's designed only to benefit Wall Street, I'll guide you through what I did in my own life beginning in the '80s and the strategies that have helped countless dentists and professionals escape the trap of never knowing how much is enough. It involves questioning the traditional approach to investing and saving for retirement. It also involves determining what's important to you and building a plan to attain those goals.

As I wrote in my book, *What's Your Next?*, designing a Freedom Blueprint™ that provides passive cash flow eliminates the worry of having to work in a practice tied to the chair or clocking in at the office. Instead, you can replace your active income with passive cash flow from alternative investments in real estate and determine how you desire to live your life right now, not some future day in retirement.

If you enjoy practicing, keep doing it! Maybe you'd like to cut back your schedule to 1 or 2 days to spend more time with your family. Or maybe you're like Dr. Andy Baber, an oral surgeon from Rogers Arkansas. While sitting in an airport heading back to the office while his family was vacationing without him, it finally hit him that there's more to life. Today, Dr. Baber has been an active part of our Freedom Founders community for four years and is one of our Free for Life™ members. Simply put, he has restructured his investment strategy and life in a way that enables him to spend quality time with his wife and his children while they're still with him!

On the other hand, you may be like Dr. Ed Hood, another one of our Free for Life™ members. Dr. Hood and his wife Gwen have been married for forty years and have three grown children, but Dr. Hood continues to show up at his practices four days a week (one day clinical, the others as business CEO) because: "It gives me purpose and it's my ministry."

Knowing the change and impact cosmetic dentistry can make on a person's life, Dr. Hood no longer views his work as drudgery or something that must be done to pay the bills. In the past, he was the dad who missed his kids' ball games because he had to be working at the office to pay the bills. Freed from the worries of income and the financial uncertainty of retirement, Ed impacts the community by performing free dental days and providing hope to patients who would normally not be able to afford the extensive cosmetic dentistry he provides. As he says, "I want my kids to know what it means to be generous. It's the legacy I want them to know."

Maybe the uncertainty of the future is causing you to work longer than you should, and your health is suffering. If so, it's time to reclaim your physical and mental health! You might be like Dr. David Scharf, who sold his practice after two years as a Freedom Founder's member. He sent me a heartfelt Christmas card describing the tears of joy he and his wife were experiencing. "You helped me realize that I had more than enough money for the rest of my life and I could take my foot off the gas and start to enjoy myself," Dr. Scharf wrote. He went on to say he had picked up his old hobby of drumming and his volunteer work as a firefighter!

This is what real freedom is all about. When you have the certainty that you "have enough" based not on accumulation but on real cash flow—cash flow that is sustainable and hedged against the ravages of inflation—then you are able to take your foot off the gas pedal and relax. Without certainty, I've witnessed countless numbers of hardworking professionals stay on the grind because of fear. That was never their goal—nor should it be for you!

It's your life, and the worries of inflation, stock market declines, or rising interest rates shouldn't be the shackles that hold you back.

You need to know that the inflation threat is real, but the good news is that inflation can be your friend, not your enemy! By preparing and taking action, you can position yourself to take advantage of the situation and propel your financial future by using the inflationary waves to push you forward. You may determine that you have enough to retire right now and enjoy the life you desire instead of waiting for—someday.

> **LEFT UNTREATED, INFLATION IS A DISEASE THAT WREAKS HAVOC ON INVESTMENTS AND RETIREMENT PLANS.**

Left untreated, inflation is a disease that wreaks havoc on investments and retirement plans.

The Layout of This Book

The Introduction lays out this book's fundamental premise and why the inflationary forces so ingrained in our monetary policy will seriously affect the citizens of our great country. In short, for the majority, we have seen the peak of the American lifestyle standard and are now on a downward spiral.

The body of the book provides a historical look at the Federal Reserve and discusses their rationale behind the monetary policy decisions that have now set the stage for inflation and the next **Great Wealth Transfer.** If you like details and analysis, you will enjoy this read.

If you are looking for actionable strategies to offset inflationary forces, jump from the Introduction to Chapter Six.

Chapter Six provides specific examples of strategies that I use myself and incorporate into our Freedom Founders Community to enable our members to create a customized Blueprint to Freedom that obviates the counter-effects of inflation and, instead, uses them to our advantage.

> **IF YOU ARE LOOKING FOR ACTIONABLE STRATEGIES TO OFFSET INFLATIONARY FORCES, JUMP FROM THE INTRODUCTION TO CHAPTER SIX.**

How We Got to Now

Most of the readers of this text have had no direct experience as adults during the last inflationary period in the U.S. (1965–1982). At the onset, I was a young teenager and an almost-graduate from Baylor College of Dentistry (now Texas A&M) in Dallas, Texas, in 1982. My first fundamental understanding of "high interest rates" came when I took my nominal earnings as a young dentist and "invested" in money market accounts at 8.5%.

I was intrigued by how much in "earnings" I could receive on my saved money. What I didn't understand then was the negative effect inflation had on that hard-earned money.

Inflation is the silent retirement killer of hopes and dreams for those unprepared.

> **INFLATION IS THE SILENT RETIREMENT KILLER OF HOPES AND DREAMS FOR THOSE UNPREPARED.**

This is precisely the trap many encounter today. Everyone loves a stimulus check or other 'free money' that the government may offer, failing to realize the strings attached. While the tax burden will continue to increase on high-income earners, the most serious battle to be fought will be with inflationary fire that has been set by the government. This fire will ravage household wealth and cause severe burdens for the retired.

A Simple Formula for Calculating the Effect of Inflation on Your Wealth

To better understand how inflation is deadly to retirement, let's first use the Rule of 72 to fully understand the impact. The Rule of 72 is a simple, back-of-the-napkin calculation to determine how quickly an investment will double. In the case of rapidly rising inflation, we can flip it around to show how quickly our wealth is decimated by the compounding effects of inflation.

Divide the interest rate into the number 72 to determine the doubling period. In this case, inflation reduces the buying power of the dollar. As I mentioned earlier, inflation is running at 7.9%, but using the 1980 CPI standards, it would be over 15%. For simple math let's make it easy. At a 12% inflation rate, a dollar today will only be worth 50 cents in 6 years (72/12% = 6 years). That means a million-dollar retirement nest egg will only buy $500K of lifestyle in 6 years. In 12 years, it's down to 25%, or $250,000. How long were you planning to live?

You understand the dilemma.

The loss of purchasing power doesn't scream at you like a loss in the stock market. You know the losses I'm talking about. Opening your statement or going online to see thousands lost to the latest stock market jitters. Watching images of planes fly into the World Trade Center and feeling that wrench in your gut, not only because of the loss of life but also because of what it would mean for your investments and future retirement plans.

> **AT A 12% INFLATION RATE, A DOLLAR TODAY WILL ONLY BE WORTH 50 CENTS IN 6 YEARS (72/12% = 6 YEARS).**

INTRODUCTION

One doctor in our group shared an emotional story of how on the same day his son was admitted to Dartmouth, all he could do was wonder how in the world he would be able to pay the tuition after losing over one million dollars during the 2008 stock market collapse.

Those losses we feel and see first-hand. Inflationary losses are real but hard to pinpoint. **That's why I call it the silent retirement killer!**

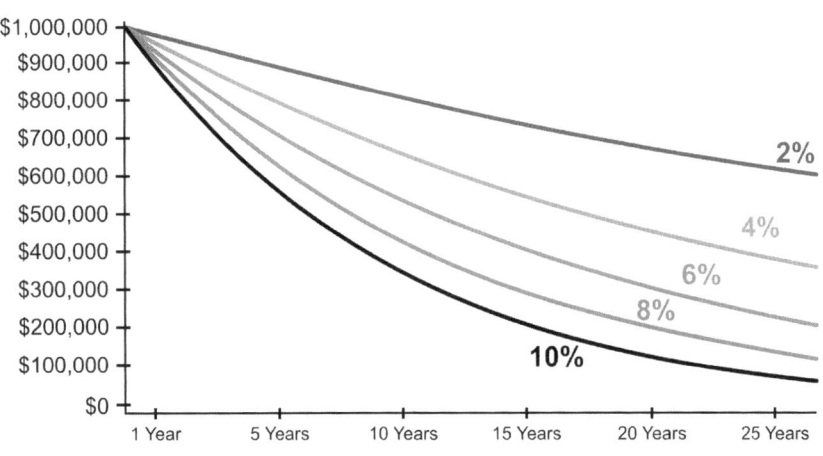

Source: Bloomberg, BBH Analysis

IT'S A NEW BALL GAME. IF YOU ARE TO WIN, YOU NEED TO GET OFF THE BENCH!

It's a new ball game. If you are to win, you need to get off the bench!

For the last forty years, the U.S. has experienced declining interest rates. From 21.5% in 1980 to 3.25% in 2022, we've been on a steep decline in interest rates. Inflation also dropped significantly from 13.5% in 1980 to less than 2% for most of the last forty years . . . until now.

Bottom line: The next decade and the decades that follow will not be a re-run of the past forty years. Whatever your plan, that model will not suffice in the years to come. And do not forget, your financial advisors, CPAs and money managers—unless they are 65 years or older—have never experienced an inflationary economy coupled with increasing interest rates.

The Secret Factors Behind the Rise of Inflation

Throughout 2021, inflation awoke. Regardless of whether you view their decision as good or bad, money well spent or money wasted, the federal government pumped $5.7 trillion into the economy from March 2020 to March 2021. On top of this, the Federal Reserve (the Fed) pumped an additional $4.7 trillion into the system by stepping up their purchase of assets to create more liquidity.

Money flooded the economy.

The Fed also lowered the reserve requirement for banks, dropped the federal funds rate to near zero (.09%) and the prime rate to 3.25%. On top of it all, the Fed has kept the prime rate at one of the lowest levels in history. We've been living under a downward trend of interest rates since 1981. Today, many people have no conceptual idea of a 30-year mortgage rate of 8%, which happens to be the historical average! Chapter Three will examine these monetary policies in depth, as they each pose unique challenges for the future.

TODAY, MANY PEOPLE HAVE NO CONCEPTUAL IDEA OF A 30-YEAR MORTGAGE RATE OF 8%, WHICH HAPPENS TO BE THE HISTORICAL AVERAGE!

INTRODUCTION

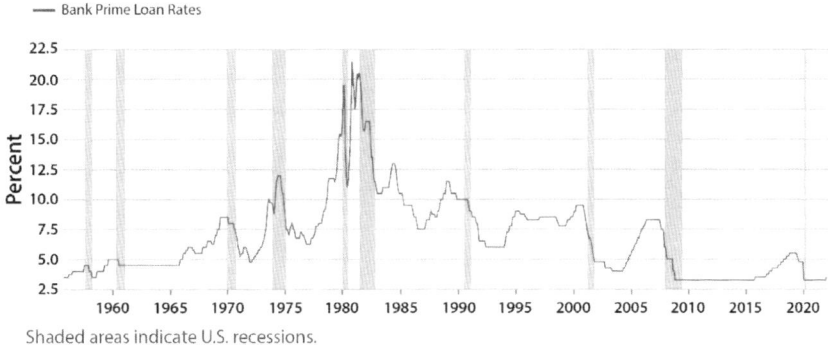

Source: Board of Governors of the Federal Reserve System (US)

What Happens When Trends Reverse?

Having a system awash in money poses a problem, but pent-up savings of households with limited places to spend is like gas slowly leaking. Eventually, it explodes. Inflation has been raging, but spending isn't near what it could be!

One look at the M1 money supply and you know we're in trouble. M1 is the amount of money readily available in checking, savings, and cash. If this chart doesn't cause your head to explode, I don't know what will.

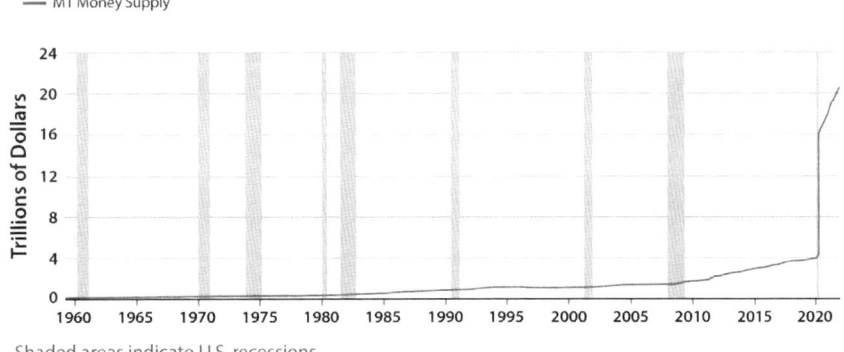

Source: Board of Governors of the Federal Reserve System (US)

Throughout 2021, new inflation reports sounded the alarm that inflation was accelerating. And every month, the Fed, the President, or the Press would insist it was an inaccurate number or that the inflation numbers were only "transitory."

"The numbers are high," they would say, "but we closed for business last year, and now we're back to work!" It made sense to the simple-minded who believe everything that officials mutter. Federal Reserve Chairman Jerome Powell finally had to walk it back on November 30, 2021, and stated that "transitory inflation" would be retired.

No Longer Transitory, Inflation Is Here to Stay

As the esteemed economist Milton Friedman argued in the '70s, "Inflation is always and everywhere a monetary phenomenon in the sense that it is and can be produced only by a more rapid increase in the quantity of money than in output."

While the Fed and government officials sang the transitory tune, the average person on the street saw it differently. Fuel prices rose 60%, beef prices 25%, used car prices 45%, and every other item increased in price by the day. Even Dollar Tree, a company with a 35-year history of selling products for $1, found itself changing course in November of 2021 by raising its prices to $1.25.

Inflation is the silent retirement killer because it gradually robs individuals of the cash they've worked to save and planned to use for retirement and their golden years.

Inflation Escalates to Levels Last Seen 40 Years Ago

For the full year of 2021, inflation leaped to 7%—the most significant jump since 1982—and as of March 2022, it was running at 7.9%. And that was prior to Russia invading Ukraine!

I want you to understand that the stage has been arranged for life-altering inflation, but I want to be precise with my language. Life-altering inflation need not become hyperinflation like that of Zimbabwe in the early 2000s or of Weimar Germany.

For perspective, 4.5 German marks were worth 1 US dollar in 1914. Four years later, it took 8.28 marks, then 46.77 in 1919, 191 marks in 1921, and finally 4.2 trillion marks in 1923!

While I don't believe it will come to that, it's obvious we're returning to the inflationary period experienced throughout the late '60s to early '80s—or even something worse.

When you throw in the aging population and high/heavy demands on Medicare and Social Security, the massive government debt, and artificially low-interest rates, alarms should be sounding in your mind.

It's also time to question some of the beliefs we've held. As you'll see throughout history, the way to stop inflation when it begins is to raise interest rates. The problem is, in doing so, the stock market will be highly vulnerable to another significant correction. (We're currently overdue for one with stock valuations looking like what Warren Buffett recently called "the mother of all stock market bubbles.")

Rising interest rates will also cause the interest on our national debt to rise, further increasing the deficit. In reality, the Fed is between a rock and a hard place. This is why you need to prepare for inflation and a significant stock market correction now.

1969 to 1982 Stock Market Returns Were Negative When Adjusted for Inflation

While I'm on the topic of the stock market, let me remind you of something Wall Street and your financial advisor won't tell you. From 1969 to 1982, cumulative inflation was 162.94%. What took $100 in 1969 required $262.94 to purchase in 1982!

For comparison, from 2007 to 2020, cumulative inflation was 24.82%. Worse yet, Wall Street will promote ads and wisdom that you must stay invested in the stock market, no matter what, to defeat inflation in your retirement savings. That's because they make money no matter what the market does!

From 1969 to 1982, the inconvenient truth is the market returned 5.3% per year but -1.8% after adjusting for inflation. Think about that.

Money invested in stocks lost 'real' purchasing value over that period. That reminds me of a story.

12.5% Interest Rates! Learning from History

A friend of mine is a real student of history. He recently shared his father's old bank certificates of deposit from the early '80s. Unfortunately, he didn't have one from the core inflationary time when things were running at 13%, but he did have one from 1982 when inflation was only 5%, and the prime rate was 16.5%. Notice how I said "only."

The CD was paying 12.5% for a 2 ½ year rate lock! **Imagine a certificate of deposit fully insured paying 12.5%!** If invested, your money would double every six years with no risk! Once again, for perspective, as I write, the prime rate is 3.25%, and a four-year CD selling at the bank is paying 0.75% to 0.90%.

When I recall that story and look at those bank certificates, it reminds me of how quickly we can forget. Psychologists say it's not our fault because our minds focus on recent times and current events instead of looking at life from a historical perspective. Recency is the psychological term, but I call it forgetting history.

Growing up and going through dental school, I used to think, "If history repeats itself, why don't people learn history and avoid those mistakes?" Rick Warren in *A Purpose Driven Church* summed it up best:

"Everything seems new if you are ignorant of history."

Today, I see it in action as support for socialism has reached new heights, especially in Millennial circles. State-controlled economies is the one economic system that has failed miserably in multiple nations and, worse yet, caused tremendous loss of life. See also: Mao's China, Stalin's USSR, and Eastern Bloc nations, plus Castro's Cuba, and Chavez's Venezuela.

But here's the real story to illustrate the way our minds operate with recency. My friend asked his father (the one with the bank CD), "Dad, why didn't you lock your money up in a U.S. Treasury for thirty years at roughly 12.5%?" His answer verbalized the psychology behind rising inflation rates that plague society and cripple economies.

We Had No Idea What Tomorrow Would Bring!

As my friend tells it, he said, "Son, you never knew where rates would go tomorrow, so you didn't want to lock it up too long."

He had lost **confidence in the currency.** Economists admit that the psychology and perspective of ordinary people on the street make controlling inflation extremely difficult. Once trust in the currency or price stability is lost, the psychology of fear takes over. From there, the fear of rising inflation feeds upon itself and engulfs the economy.

The good news is, as my mentor and co-author of *Own Your Freedom: Sustainable Wealth for a Volatile World*, Dan S. Kennedy, says,

"There's always opportunity in times of crisis." And that's what I want you to remember as I take you through where we're at and where we're most likely heading.

Don't bury your head in the ground or buy into the groupthink and conventional wisdom that everything is fine! It's essential for survival to act and think differently! You must be the radar searching the sky for danger.

Doors of great opportunities will open by taking action to identify where we're heading and implementing a plan that has been proven to work during times of rapidly rising inflation.

As the economy was crumbling during the Great Depression and people were jumping from buildings, others made tons of money and succeeded. Since I'm a massive believer in real estate, many people naturally ask, "How much did you lose during the 2008 mortgage meltdown?"

My answer goes right back to what I mentioned above: "There's always opportunity in times of crisis." I doubled my net worth during that time.

How could I succeed and do so well during those tough times when so many were destroyed? I had an entire network of people around me who always looked at life differently. Being a contrarian and full of curiosity, I'm constantly evaluating market conditions, societal factors, and economic cycles. I've trained my mind to view things differently, just as this book will do for you.

Develop your mind to ask questions. Ponder and critically examine information. Most importantly, surround yourself with people who think and act differently than the masses.

Observe, Plan, and Skate to Where the Puck Is Going

> *For more specific strategies and tactics on negating the effects of inflation, go to Chapter Six.*

I can't stress this enough. Even in the worst of times, look for opportunities. Wayne Gretsky is an excellent lesson for us during this journey. The hockey community knows him as "The Great One." He was undoubtedly a fantastic player, but what struck me was his answer to a question about what made him so great. He said, "I skate to where the puck is going, not to where it's been."

If you've watched Gretsky, he seemed to intuitively know where the puck was heading and how he should approach the situation. This was ingrained in his thought process. Our thought process needs to be the same. Skate to where the puck is going!

But beware. **Your greatest enemy is groupthink and conventional wisdom.**

Groupthink is a dangerous plague that has eviscerated society. It takes hold because we go along with the crowds without questioning the truth. We shy away from thinking opposite the crowd because we want to fit in. Social media has exacerbated the problem as Big Tech dictates reality. I've always felt sorry for the Chinese whose internet is filtered by what the Communist Party will allow them to see.

Today, our social media and internet are filtered by Big Tech. No matter what side of the aisle you sit on, anyone with an open mind can understand how dangerous it is when large companies and the government control thought and information.

Develop that inner desire to evaluate everything with your own eyes. Ask the tough questions and get around others who will challenge you.

I'll share with you strategies to stay ahead of inflation.

Throughout the book, I'll share examples of how to whip inflation, including owning real, tangible assets like a business or real estate. Owning a business allows you to increase revenues as inflation increases, as you can adjust your prices.

No doubt it takes prudence and wisdom in handling accounts receivables and negotiating accounts payable terms from vendors, but it's a solid strategy. The business environment is often robust during inflation because consumers are motivated to spend before prices rise tomorrow! Every day is a deal because tomorrow the costs will be higher!

Real estate, though, is my favorite.

As you'll learn, real estate has been the only tangible investment asset to keep up with inflation. As an investor in real estate (vs. an active business), I can invest passively and enjoy more TIME—which was the point of my working hard in my younger years.

If I can't buy back my TIME well before the societal "retirement age" of 65, then I've completely missed the mark.

> IF I CAN'T BUY BACK MY TIME WELL BEFORE THE SOCIETAL "RETIREMENT AGE" OF 65, THEN I'VE COMPLETELY MISSED THE MARK.

If you haven't followed me on social media or haven't read my other books, you'll learn I was a successful young dentist and I had my own plans to build both my practice and real estate business. All that changed in 1994 when my daughter, Jenna, was diagnosed with high-risk acute lymphocytic leukemia at age two. After undergoing multiple rounds of chemotherapy, she began having epileptic seizures. In 2004, when she was twelve years old, she had a severe episode that left her vomiting blood on the floor. She was airlifted to Dallas, and three days later, she was diagnosed with end-stage liver failure. At that point, Jenna was placed on an organ transplant list, and we waited.

If you've ever dealt with the anxiety and stress of a loved one suffering, you understand. Life was in constant upheaval, and I felt powerless. You want to do something to help, but you can't.

In August 2004, I received "the call" at my office. "Dr. Phelps, I've got good news for you." We learned a liver was available, and Jenna was rushed to surgery. As I sat in the waiting room and prayed, all these thoughts went through my head. Would she survive the operation? Would the liver transplant work? It was totally out of my control.

The Questions That Raced through My Mind

I did a lot of thinking as I sat there waiting. I questioned my own life as I prayed for her. How many choices had I made unconsciously? How many times did work take me away from spending time with her? How could I reclaim control of my life and my choices? How could I make my family's lives better? How could I live a life of no regrets?

I even questioned the traditional mindset. Was I going to build a life that afforded me the freedom of time with my daughter, or would I continue on the traditional path and give away my time to the career and business I had spent decades building?

> **HOW MANY TIMES DID WORK TAKE ME AWAY FROM SPENDING TIME WITH HER?**

Six hours later, the surgeon came out and reported that the operation was a success! My child was going to survive! Yes, challenging days were ahead, but I knew Jenna had the tenacity and courage to fight as she always had.

I'm thankful for those hours sitting in the waiting room because they changed my life forever. I made a commitment never to view my finances, career, or personal goals in the same way. That day was a wake-up call, and I decided to live life under my terms and conditions.

Thanks to strategies I had put into place in the years prior, building a portfolio of alternative investments in real estate, I was able to sell my practice and reorganize my life. I then focused on what mattered most—spending time with my daughter. Today I lead a collaborative group of dentists and healthcare and business professionals in the Freedom Founders Community, and we recreate the same outcome in other people's lives.

> *For more specific strategies and tactics on negating the effects of inflation, go to Chapter Six.*

At Freedom Founders, we prioritize how we desire to live our lives, and we create financial freedom utilizing strategies found outside of Wall Street. Throughout the book, I'll be sharing stories and examples from my clients and colleagues who have escaped the traditional mindset. They've made a decision to ignore what Wall Street says and what society dictates as the norm. Instead, they've built a life on their own terms and conditions. That is true freedom!

The entire premise is built on replicating or replacing one's active, labor-produced income by using alternative investments in real estate. That's financial freedom! But how does one get there? What does that mean? How risky is this model?

It begins by determining your Freedom Number™, which determines how much you need in monthly cash flow to replace your active income. The next step is to reverse engineer from that number to determine "how much equity" you should need invested at a specific return to reach your Freedom Number™. With the forces of inflation working for you, you'll escape the trap of worrying when or if you can retire. Instead, you'll have a focused plan, no matter what life throws at you.

One of our Freedom Founders members, Dr. Dennis Perry, worried about having enough to retire, but after 31 years of practicing as an oral surgeon, his body had been worn down. "After multiple surgeries on my neck and back, coupled with the stress and responsibility of having people's lives in my hands, it was time to call it quits and for me to spend time with my sweetheart." Following the traditional constructs of retirement planning, Dennis and his wife Monzell were concerned (as were many) in March of 2020 when the market crashed. It couldn't have come at a worse time for Dennis because he had just retired at the end of 2019. Searching for clarity and guidance in retirement, Dennis and Monzell joined Freedom Founders in the summer of 2020.

During one of our Blueprint meetings in January, Dennis told the small group how his cash flow came like clockwork in his various real estate investments, and his principal kept growing. It kept growing even though he earned enough passive cash flow to live the life he and Monzell wanted to live! His only regrets were not knowing these concepts in alternative investments earlier in life.

Today, Dennis and Monzell are Free for Life, and they play an important role in the Freedom Founders Community, serving as a resource for other members. They've even stepped up by helping lead weekly accountability calls with other members. As Dennis said, "A mentor of mine told me, true freedom is doing what you want, when you want, where you want, and with whom you want. Of course, that mentor was you, David!"

But Isn't Real Estate Risky?

The sad truth is most investors are only aware of Wall Street-type real estate products like REITs or purchasing something locally as a rental home. Believe me, those are risky! In the case of rental properties, many who acquire properties soon find they've created a second job for themselves—hunting for bargains, closing, repairing, renting. Worse yet, many savvy professionals, unfamiliar with real estate, invest in the wrong properties in the wrong areas. They're unfamiliar with how to deal with tenants or even management companies who fleece you at every turn. This is a risky strategy!

Sadly, I see it every day. The local real estate group is "coming to your area" to sell investing in rental properties programs. The hidden secret is that there are various aspects of real estate investing that the public has absolutely no idea about and are only available to investors with higher net worth.

If you're interested in learning how other dentists and professional practice owners are utilizing strategies such as these, check out a pre-recorded webinar I recently led on this very topic. You can find it at **www.InflationBookResources.com**.

What I really love about real estate is that it allows investors to leverage, lock in fixed costs with long-term mortgages, and adjust cash flow. It's also the one item, besides food, that a household needs to survive.

Realize there are many aspects of real estate, so don't get caught up in your "vision" of real estate. It's more than buying a rental and dealing with tenants and toilets. For many dentists and professional practice owners with whom I work at Freedom Founders, the last thing they desire is a second job managing tenants and contractors!

Real estate should be passive and diversified into various alternative investments in real estate. More importantly, it should produce consistent and sustainable cash flow (like the goose and the golden eggs).

But living life under our terms and conditions requires active participation and personal responsibility. We can't be naive, and we can't abdicate to others—even so-called professional advisors and money managers. Silent killers and dangers to our future are out there, lurking around dark corners. The real question is "What will you do about it?"

With inflation rapidly rising to levels not seen in forty years, the words of John Maynard Keynes, written in his book, *The Economic Consequences of the Peace*, ring in my ears.

"By a continuing process of inflation, the government can confiscate, secretly and unobserved, an important part of the wealth of their citizens."

What About the Traditional 60/40 Stocks to Bonds Portfolio? Will It Work?

During inflationary times, stock market investments do not keep up with inflation. Contrary to what Wall Street will tell you, from 1969 to 1982, stock market returns were 5.3% per year but -1.8% adjusted for inflation. Most financial advisors providing advice today have never experienced inflation of this magnitude.

Worse yet, Wall Street advises transitioning to fixed income as we age to reduce volatility and potential losses from the stock market. Losses, especially in the early years of retirement, sabotage hopes and dreams. The general rule has been to construct a portfolio based on 60% stocks and 40% bonds, then shift to 40% stocks and 60% bonds, eventually reaching a 30/70 blend for income and capital preservation in retirement.

For years, that strategy might have worked when bonds were paying 6–9%. However, since 2008 and the lowering of interest rates to rock bottom levels, yields on bond portfolios have returned next to nothing. Try living on fixed income paying 2–4%! Worse yet, with inflation at 7.9%, the real return on bonds is negative! In response to historically low interest rates, advisors have "chased yield and returns," which has forced investors into portfolios with greater stock exposure. That has only amplified risk.

On the other side, investors who have purchased bonds for safety and security are set to be slaughtered. It's such a risk that the Securities and Exchange Commission recently published an investor bulletin warning: "Interest Rate Risk—When Interest Rates Go Up, Prices of Fixed-Rate Bonds Fall" (SEC Publication No. 151).

As interest rates rise, bondholders lose value. A portfolio with $100,000 in fixed income paying 3% and coming due in 10 years will lose $7,500 in principal if rates rise only 1% (and that's if it's a U.S. Treasury backed by the printing press). Corporate bonds or worse yet, high yield "junk bonds" will fall even further. What happens if rates rise back to normal levels of 6–8%?

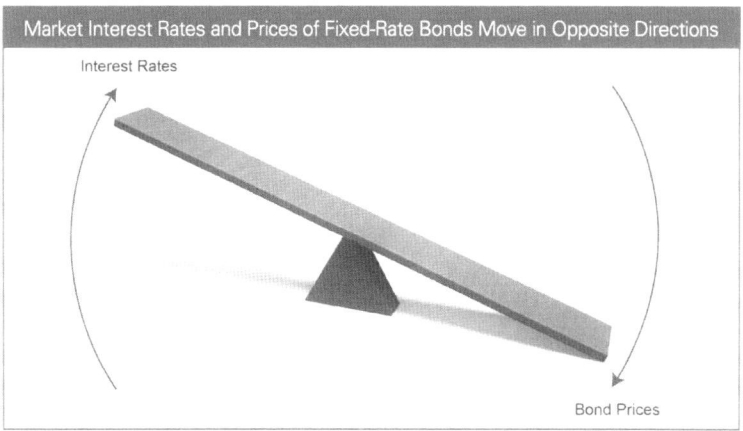

Let History Be Your Guide: There's Nothing New under the Sun

In closing, my goal and promise are to position you to win no matter what inflation does by implementing the strategies and ideas I share. Every season has a cycle. First, we'll learn how inflation begins. Next, we'll examine the tsunami of inflation ahead, which can silently kill retirement and life savings. Then we'll build our arc to survive the storm. Just like an arc that uses the flooding waters to "float," you'll learn how to use the rising tide of inflation to propel your retirement.

In the book of Ecclesiastes, King Solomon notes "What has been will be again, what has been done will be done again; there is nothing new under the sun."

As I guide you through history, I'll remind you where we've been. The good news is that we've faced difficulties and calamities throughout history. We've dealt with Covid-type diseases, global warming (a little thing called the Medieval Warming Period), wars, economic struggles, and much more. We can win and protect our family and even our community with the courage to act. Will the battle be tough? Absolutely. Can you do it? For sure!

Keep always the quote by the Spanish philosopher George Santayana who said, "Those who cannot remember the past are condemned to repeat it."

History has already provided a guide and a map to victory over inflation. Let's put it into practice!

To Your Freedom!

> *For specific strategies and tactics on negating the effects of inflation, go to Chapter Six.*

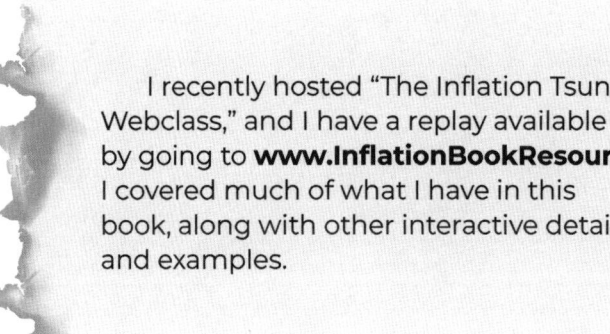

I recently hosted "The Inflation Tsunami Webclass," and I have a replay available for you by going to **www.InflationBookResources.com**. I covered much of what I have in this book, along with other interactive details and examples.

A PRIMER ON MONEY & CONFISCATION

CHAPTER ONE

> For more specific strategies and tactics on negating the effects of inflation, go to Chapter Six.

"Paper money eventually returns to its intrinsic value—zero."
VOLTAIRE, FRENCH WRITER

"Government is the only institution that can take a valuable commodity like paper, and make it worthless by applying ink"
LUDWIG VON MISES, AUSTRIAN ECONOMIST

"The history of paper money is an account of abuse, mismanagement, and financial disaster."
RICHARD EBELING, PROFESSOR AT THE CITADEL

To understand the dangers we face in the next ten years, a basic understanding of the origins of inflation is paramount. Inflation shows up in prices and wages, but the root cause is an increase in a nation's currency.

Price stability results from currency stability which is vital for economic stability. Among nations that have crumbled, they similarly have suffered from a debasement of their currencies.

Vladimir Lenin expressed the goal of Marxism to defeat capitalism when he wrote, "The best way to destroy the capitalistic system is to debauch the currency." The Marxists believed that a debauched currency would hold no value and, thus, would eliminate the profit motive. Making the Proletariat and the Bourgeoisie equal was the ultimate goal of the Marxists.

Unfortunately, the Communists and Marxists haven't had to lift a finger because our politicians have done it for them! In a series of steps that began in the late '60s, our government has overspent and overpromised, causing us to face disastrous consequences. But to be honest, we're also to blame as stakeholders in the U.S. economy.

The truth is, we've grown accustomed to wanting money from the government. Money for schools, roads, and bridges. Money for our state and local communities.

You might not remember, or maybe you weren't even born, when after the U.S.S.R. collapsed President Clinton proposed a plan for military base closures. Every official seemed to agree, and everyone spoke of the "peace dividend" from a reduction in military spending. The problem was that everyone wanted bases closed *in other states but not theirs!* Those bases meant federal dollars flowing into their community.

> **LEFT UNTREATED, INFLATION IS A DISEASE THAT WREAKS HAVOC ON INVESTMENTS AND RETIREMENT PLANS.**

It brings me back to the universal truth of money. "Easy money and overspending are like alcohol," the economist Milton Friedman said. "It feels good initially, but too much of it causes problems. When the problems come, and there will be problems, taking the pain is too harsh, so it's masked over, and the can is kicked down the road."

Money Is the Root of All Evil: When You Don't Control It

Most people have a basic understanding of money, but it's extremely limited. We use money to buy or sell goods and services from others worldwide, while bartering is used on a limited scale to trade products with others.

A farmer who trades beef to a local merchant who makes clothes eventually determines that the merchant needs more beef than the farmer needs clothes. Now what? The merchant needs beef to eat, but the farmer doesn't need more clothes.

Money allows the farmer to sell his beef, attain money from the merchant, and then use it to purchase other goods or services. Various cultures have placed different monetary values on items for their mercantile purposes. Rock salt was currency in Ethiopia, brass rings in West Africa, gold dust in the North American west, and tobacco in the early American colonies. These were all forms of what we would call currency or money.

Money is simply something that society has chosen to value.

Tobacco as Currency

As Friedman discussed in the PBS series *Free to Choose* in 1980, "A funny thing happens when a value is attached to an item. People begin to produce more of it! It doesn't matter if it's paper money, coins, or tobacco."

In the 1600s, tobacco was the currency of the Carolinas and the early colonies. Like any item used as society's currency, the price of tobacco rose uncontrollably fast as it was produced in mass. Friedman points out, "At the end of the process, prices were forty times higher... and as always when inflation occurs, people complained. As always, elected officials tried to do something and, as always, to very little avail."

Typical of government wisdom, the legislatures changed the laws, set production limits, instituted control, and even dictated who could produce tobacco. They went so far as to squeeze out producers they didn't like while allowing others, whom the lawmakers favored, to grow more.

Poor quality tobacco was used to pay debts while good tobacco was shipped and sold. These actions tarnished the quality, which drove down the value of tobacco as currency. But this was no isolated incident and has occurred throughout the centuries when fiat currency is used.

The Roman Empire

Emperor Constantine (reigned AD 306–337) is considered one of the most significant Roman Emperors. Still the economy crumbled at his feet as inflation soared, taxes increased, and the concentration of wealth caused riots and chaos. Of course, there was also massive corruption!

While history places the defeat of the Roman Empire to the Germanic Tribes, the real culprit was overspending, corruption, waste, an overstretched army, and most importantly, inflation.

Throughout the history of the Roman Empire, the makeup of the coins constantly changed to include fewer and fewer precious metals. Every new emperor overspent and, to pay for it, debased the currency by changing the composition of the coins.

Under Diocletian (AD 284–305), the Denarius had gone from 95–98% pure silver under Caesar Augustus to a copper coin with silver coating. The Roman Empire is a case study of how inflation and overspending collapse an economy and world power—no matter how great they are.

It's Not Worth a Continental

Fast forward to the United States in 1775. Our nation encountered rampant inflation when the Continental Congress issued currency to finance the Revolutionary War. Called Continentals, this fiat money lacked any exchange rate with precious metals or hard assets. With no limit on printing, printing is what they did! Shortly after, inflation skyrocketed.

Historians note that a common saying in the colonies for inferior products in those days was, "It's not worth a continental." The fiat money had become worthless.

The United States of America

Learning from history, the newly created United States, in 1792, minted coins under the Mint Act, which were backed by hard assets. The coins operated without incident, but the issuing entity, the First Bank of the United States, was only allowed a twenty-year charter of operation, which wasn't renewed.

In its place rose individual banks issuing currency backed by their assets. Before the Civil War, nearly 1,600 banknotes floated around the nation. Interstate commerce was challenging because everyone had their own unique currency, which constrained the economy.

Then the Civil War began. To fund the Civil War in 1861, the federal government began to issue "greenbacks" backed by the full faith and credit of the United States. Like the Continentals, Greenbacks were fiat money, and as always, inflation soared 14% in 1862, and 25% in 1863 and 1864 as the printing presses ran unchecked. The spiral continued until President Grant pushed for Greenbacks to be backed by gold, which they became in 1869 under the Public Credit Act.

In 1873, the nation was rocked by a significant downturn largely tied to railroad credit and investments. Interestingly enough, during the panic, the Greenback Labor Party grew in momentum as members, particularly farmers, pushed for the return of the Greenback to fiat currency, no longer backed by gold.

Why the desire for fiat money? Farmers were in debt on loans, and **inflation was their friend**, decreasing their "effective debt" and raising prices!

> FARMERS WERE IN DEBT ON LOANS, AND INFLATION WAS THEIR FRIEND, DECREASING THEIR "EFFECTIVE DEBT" AND RAISING PRICES!

That's a great lesson to keep in mind as we move forward. When inflation occurs, debts become cheaper because you're paying for the fixed debt with inflated dollars. That is why in times of inflation, a major goal must be to secure your debts with long-term fixed interest rates.

The right debt can be your friend in inflationary times, but it can be a brutal enemy if it's adjustable. I'll discuss this more in Chapter Six.

Creation of the Federal Reserve

In 1913, the Federal Reserve was created, and it became the Central Bank of the United States. Initially, it was formed as an independent, private member bank unbeholden to the government but responsible for balancing monetary policy with economic conditions and public sentiment. Some might argue today if the Fed is indeed independent.

In 1914, the Fed issued its first Federal Reserve Notes or dollars as we know them today. Initially, all money was linked to the gold standard at **$20.67 an ounce.** That meant that at any time, you could trade an ounce of gold for $20.67 or vice versa. Naturally, the goal was to prevent the government from printing more money than what it owned in gold.

Gold Confiscation by FDR

During the Great Depression, the nation lost confidence in the economy and the banking system. Bank runs were commonplace, and general uncertainty surrounded the country. All the while, nearly 9,000 banks closed between 1930 and 1933. Due to this, many citizens exchanged their reserve notes for gold for its safety.

English author, George Bernard Shaw, summed it up best when he was asked: Who do you trust more gold or politicians? He reportedly said, "You have a choice of trusting the natural stability of gold or the honesty and intelligence of members of government."

As we've seen many times in U.S. history, the federal government has a long reach into the lives of average citizens, and it has continued to grow in power. In 1933, President Franklin Delano Roosevelt outlawed the holding of gold by individuals to stop the draining of the United States gold reserve. It was confiscation on a mass scale to eliminate a run on the gold supply. Under the Gold Reserve Act, confiscated gold was exchanged at **$20.67 an ounce**.

For a time, the currency floated, untethered to gold, as the nation's banking system reorganized and restructured. Shockingly, in 1934, the country returned to the gold standard but at a new price of **$35 an ounce**! Talk about a return on your investment!

The government bought the gold for $20.67 an ounce, then set a new price at $35! This single move inflated the value of the gold by nearly 70%, which in turn allowed the currency to be inflated. It reminds me of the adage: When there's a will, there's a way!

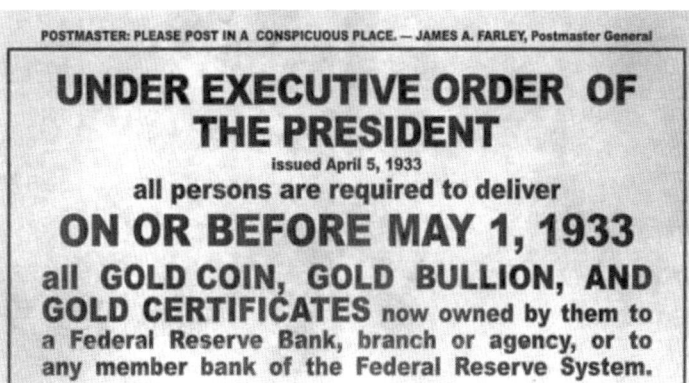

Cryptocurrency: Could History Repeat?

Be warned. I'm skeptical about cryptocurrency or gold as alternatives, and this part of American history is why I'm particularly cautious of such actions. Governments are dependent on citizens having faith and using the nation's currency.

It also requires citizens to use nothing else as currency. Having had a history of confiscation right here in the U.S. within the last 100 years is a wake-up call.

Who's to say it won't happen again? Kind of like the shutdowns we experienced during Covid. Who would have imagined those shutdowns two months earlier! Freedom must be fought for and defended because liberty and its erosion are typically slow.

However, I believe that when push comes to shove economically, cryptocurrency and other items that serve as an alternative to the U.S. Dollar will not be allowed to stand. Maybe they won't confiscate it, but they'll tax the hell out of it.

Regardless, the government will attempt to regulate cryptocurrencies. President Biden recently sought to significantly tax and treat crypto trading differently than other investments. The rule changes proposed would have had substantial regulatory implications for average citizens, which before now were only required of brokerage firms.

Let's face it. If gold or crypto threatens the future of the government printing money, then it's a target, as we saw in 1933! The United States owes nearly $30 trillion and requires new purchasers of U.S. debt monthly.

Will an alternative currency be allowed to grow in demand and power? How many even know the history behind the confiscation of gold in the '30s? If it happened once, it could happen again.

Please step back and look at the power grab we've seen from Covid. What about other western nations now preventing the un-vaccinated from leaving their homes (i.e., Australia and Switzerland). It doesn't even need to be the United States that takes action against Bitcoin; it could be

China, Japan, or England. There's a risk that no one is even discussing or thinking about it.

"Wait," the crypto people will say. "El Salvador is now accepting Bitcoin!" Yes, it is, but their entire economy is $24 billion, roughly what the U.S. spends monthly on interest payments. For a bit of perspective, every state in the union has a higher GDP than El Salvador. It's nothing, so don't get too excited about it.

Now, let's get back to our monetary journey.

Bretton Woods Agreement 1944

Following World War II, the United States and other free nations formed the Bretton Woods Agreement in 1944. The agreement made the U.S. Dollar supreme since it was tied to gold, and other countries pegged their currency to the dollar for price stability. This agreement brought stability to the free world until the U.S. began overspending in the 1960s. Can you imagine that? The U.S. government overspending?

First, President Lyndon Baines Johnson "LBJ" pursued his Great Society programs, including Medicare, Medicaid, and his war on poverty. Next, the Vietnam War escalated, with over 550,000 soldiers sent to Vietnam by 1968, and due to these budgetary expenditures, the United States began to run enormous deficits. The highest since WWII, totaling **$25 billion**.

Don't confuse "deficit" and "debt." Deficit spending is the excess yearly spending of the United States, and if the nation runs a deficit, it then increases the national debt. Politicians and spin masters love to confuse and confound, so please pay careful attention to the difference between debt and deficit.

In present-day dollars, $25 billion in deficit spending would be equivalent to almost $200 billion. That's how far out of whack we've gone. Today, a budget deficit of $1 trillion passes without hesitation, but $200 billion in today's dollars lit the fire for the inflation that would take hold in the late '60s and '70s and introduced a new term: **Stagflation**.

In the '60s, politicians from both aisles were concerned about the staggering deficit and how to get it under control. Today, nobody cares about deficit spending.

A new economic theory has even arisen—Modern Monetary Theory (MMT). This theory states that if you have the keys to the printing press, you can always print as much money as you want with no side effects! I'll touch on that in a little because MMT is gaining traction with progressive lawmakers and society.

In 1966, debt was a serious issue because the currency was tied to gold! Naturally, it all began to collapse. A 2014 study by the International Monetary Funds entitled, "Money Matters—The Incredible Shrinking Gold Supply," notes that foreign banks held nearly $14 billion in U.S. dollars. The problem was there was only $13.2 billion of gold bullion in reserve. All but $3.2 billion was available for foreign banks, with the remaining reserves devoted to the U.S.

CHAPTER ONE: A PRIMER ON MONEY & CONFISCATION

The government had cheated! Can you believe it? The U.S. had printed more than it should have and had pumped up the money supply to cover the cost of spending programs and the war.

The Death of the Gold Standard

Chapter Three examines the '60s, the '70s, and '80s, but for a monetary overview, President Nixon stuck a fork in gold-based currency in August 1971 by removing the United States from the gold standard.

The government could now print as much as it desired with the currency only backed by the full faith and credit of the United States.

Without gold backing the currency, politicians from both parties ran the printing press full speed, leading to the nearly $30 trillion owed today. The chart below sums it all up in one image.

Pay particular attention to 2008 on the chart. The 2008 financial crisis is a small jump on the chart compared to what has been happening ever since and especially recently. Inflation has landed on our shores for this very reason. Too many dollars are chasing too few goods—Economics 101.

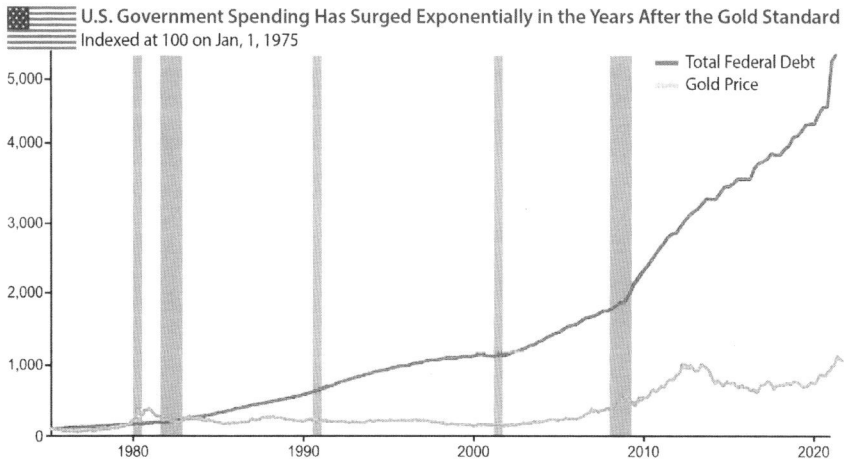

Source: IBA, Treasury Department, U.S. Global Investors

www.InflationBook.com ■ 11

Once again, Milton Friedman's wisdom rings true. "Inflation is only made in one place. The Printing Press."

One of my favorite lessons from scripture is in the Gospels when Jesus says that you could know the season by observing the leaves on a fig tree.

The leaves on my fig tree that I examine carefully in this season are the numbers, actions, and underlying forces driving inflation coupled with Federal Reserve actions and monetary policy. Let us now begin to understand how and where inflation shows up in our lives.

Visit **www.InflationBookResources.com** to access additional information and resources. There are interviews with thought-leaders on inflation, investments, the future, and much more. It's free of charge and my gift to you for investing in your future!

CHAPTER TWO

INFLATION & HOW IT SHOWS UP IN OUR LIVES

> *If you are looking for actionable strategies to offset inflationary forces, jump to Chapter Six.*

> *"Inflation is like a sin; every government denounces it and every government practices it."*
> **FREDERICK LEITH-ROSS, SCOTTISH ECONOMIST**

> *"I do not think it is an exaggeration to say history is largely a history of inflation, usually inflations engineered by governments for the gain of governments."*
> **FRIEDRICH HAYEK, AUSTRIAN-BRITISH ECONOMIST**

Having explored the creation and destruction of currency throughout time, we now shift focus to how inflation shows up in the economy. To prepare for the upcoming tidal wave of inflation, a lesson in how it manifests is required.

Simply put, inflation is too many dollars chasing too few goods. That in turn, causes the price of goods to increase. Micro- and macro-economics courses in colleges devote large swaths of their text to supply and demand. Too many widgets and not enough demand—the price falls. More demand than the supply of widgets—the price rises to reach equilibrium.

It seems as if most of our ruling class failed to enroll in economics class because the idea of setting minimum wages at certain levels or forcing price controls are sure-fire ways to fuel inflation.

Worse yet, wanting to spend an additional $3.5 trillion in printed money, as the country is already suffering from rising inflation, is a recipe for disaster. Thankfully, the Build Back Better plan looks dead—for now. But the one constant we know is this: politicians love to spend money. To read the fig leaves, as I mentioned earlier, understanding the types of inflationary factors is vital.

Demand-Pull Inflation

Demand-pull inflation occurs when the money supply increases, either by the printing of money or by the Fed lowering interest rates and performing asset purchases, creating money out of thin air. The nearly $5.7 trillion of pandemic relief spending coupled with $4.7 trillion from the Fed's balance sheet that flooded the economy since the Covid pandemic began is example #1 of demand-pull inflation. In Chapter Five, "Inflation Roars Back to Life", we'll examine our current inflationary pressure caused by demand-pull.

More money to spend drives demand for products and services, which drives up prices. Because our economy is so consumer-driven, demand-pull inflation can lead to serious inflation.

Contributing factors not shown on the chart below are the growth of emerging economies and their demand for resources. As China and India experience rapid growth, the global economy requires enormous allotments of lumber, concrete, copper, plastics—the list goes on and on. China's growth has been somewhat staggering ever since the U.S. allowed its entrance into the World Trade Organization.

CAUSES OF INFLATION

```
              CUT IN
           INTEREST RATES
                 ↓
   HIGHER → DEMAND-PULL ← INCREASED
   WAGES     INFLATION    MONEY SUPPLY
         ↘
           COST-PUSH
           INFLATION   ← INFLATION
         ↗               EXPECTATIONS
   DEVALUATION
```

This growth leads to a worldwide demand-pull. Look no further than automobiles. Twenty years ago, Chinese citizens didn't have cars except for the ruling class. Today they're the largest auto market. Remember when oil went over **$140 a barrel** in 2008? Yes, it was due to the dollar becoming less valuable, but China was also consuming more oil, and fracking in the U.S. hadn't yet ramped up to meet the demand.

Cost-Push Inflation

Today, politicians talk about supply-side issues causing our current inflation; however, supply fits in on the cost-push side of the equation. I'll remind you, politicians love to look for a boogeyman to blame instead of looking at themselves, so be on the lookout for their games.

They begin trotting out "suspects" who are taking advantage of people and are raising prices. Then they'll start to call for price gouging investigations. The government prints too much money, debases the currency, and then looks for someone to blame. We've seen this story play out throughout history.

This strategy is a core aspect of Marxist revolutionaries. They drive public support to nationalize or take over private industries that are targeted for "taking advantage of" the population.

Today, President Biden has launched an investigation into oil and gas companies and meat processors, blaming them for the rising gas and food prices. The Department of Justice recently announced they were looking at monopoly, antitrust violations against meat packers. But remember, to get to where they're at today, the government had to allow them to consolidate and purchase other meat packers. With the crisis in Ukraine sending oil prices to levels not seen since 2008 and prices at the pump jumping over 47% from one year ago, the government has called for investigations into price gouging. But who is really to blame?

In Chapter Four, we'll examine how the Arab Oil Embargo sent shockwaves through America as the Organization of the Petroleum Exporting Countries (OPEC) nations stopped selling oil to the supporters of Israel. Due to the price controls instituted under Nixon, domestic drillers were driven out of business or reduced capacity causing a supply issue.

In 2007 we experienced the same thing as demand grew and supply slowed from the OPEC nations. This was a catalyst for the great recession when prices skyrocketed and threatened the economy. Since that time, domestic drillers revolutionized their exploration process via fracking, and reduced regulation under President Trump led to a historic turnaround in the energy sector for America.

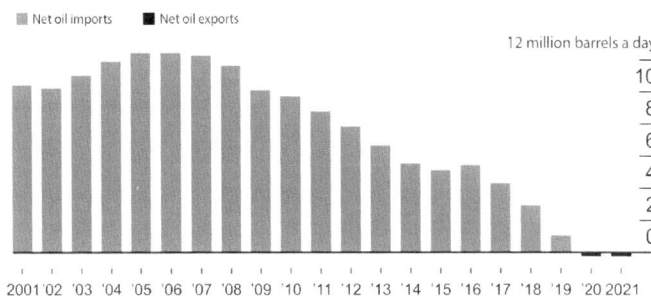

Source: U.S. Energy Information Administration
Note: Includes crude oil and refined products

In 2021, the first action by the Biden Administration was to kill the Keystone XL Pipeline, which would have brought oil from Canada, and to cease new drilling on federal lands while raising lease rates on existing wells.

But it gets worse. President Biden nominated Sarah Bloom Raskin to the Federal Reserve Board of Governors. Raskin has argued that banks should cease lending to oil and gas companies to address global warming while being championed as a regulator who will focus on climate change within the financial system. He also nominated, Saule Omarova, for the Office of Comptroller of the Currency, who has said she wants oil and gas companies to go bankrupt to tackle climate change. I call it like it is. **Oil and gas companies are in the crosshairs**. That will mean higher fuel prices which leads to higher food prices which leads to higher inflation.

Many "blue states," such as Vermont, New York, and Maryland, have even begun clamping down on fracking. As we'll see, decreased supply leads to increased prices. We're now importing oil again, which is sad to see considering what we had accomplished as a nation and the crisis in the Ukraine is revealing what happens when we're dependent on others for energy.

> OIL AND GAS COMPANIES ARE IN THE CROSSHAIRS. THAT WILL MEAN HIGHER FUEL PRICES WHICH LEADS TO HIGHER FOOD PRICES WHICH LEADS TO HIGHER INFLATION.

Rising Labor Costs Leads to Higher Inflation

Another factor of cost-push inflation is wages. During previous generations, labor unions controlled over 30% of the labor market compared to roughly 10% today. As inflation spiraled in the '70s, unions fought for significant wage increases to maintain living standards, often resorting to strikes.

After contracts were negotiated, companies raised prices and carried costs through to the consumer, pushing inflation higher. This was met with disdain from the public, who called for wage freezes to limit the power of unions. This hasn't appeared today due to low union membership, but a twist has occurred.

Before the Covid pandemic, the economy was operating at full capacity with 3.5% unemployment, the lowest since 1968, and over eight million unfilled positions in February 2020. Today there are nearly 11 million job openings, with almost four million workers yet to return to work from pre-pandemic levels, thus exacerbating the limited supply of labor.

Cost-push inflation has led to a 10% increase in average hourly earnings and a quit rate of over 3%. The quit rate is a statistic famously used by former Fed Chairman Alan Greenspan that tracks people leaving one job and moving to another. Three percent is the highest on record! Like the unions of the '70s pushing for higher wages, today's workers are demanding higher wages which is driving significant cost-push inflation.

Finally, we come to the deadliest influencer of cost-push inflation: **Inflation expectations and psychology**.

Paper money requires confidence for stability. When faith is lost or people anticipate increased prices, inflation feeds upon itself. Instead of postponing purchases, buyers move forward with their purchases, believing it will cost more tomorrow. One of President Gerald Ford's strategies against inflation was to encourage Americans to pledge not to purchase anything unless it was an absolute necessity, in an effort to drive down prices with diminished demand.

Naturally, it caused the opposite effect, and people rushed out to purchase more out of fear. It reminds me of the toilet paper crisis during the Covid pandemic!

CHAPTER TWO: INFLATION & HOW IT SHOWS UP IN OUR LIVES

As fear of higher prices takes hold, the demand-pull side of the inflation equation increases and drives prices higher, reinforcing in the consumers' minds that they were right. A classic positive feedback loop.

Because of this factor, the Federal Reserve closely monitors various aspects of the economy, including consumer sentiment, to determine which strategies they might implement to either inflate or deflate the money supply.

That leads us to the Fed's strategies and techniques to inflate or deflate the economy and achieve its goals.

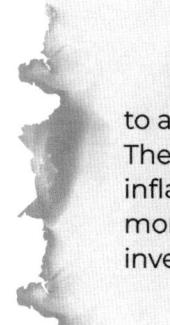

Visit **www.InflationBookResources.com** to access additional information and resources. There are interviews with thought-leaders on inflation, investments, the future, and much more. It's free of charge and my gift to you for investing in your future!

MONETARY POLICY & TECHNIQUES OF THE FED

CHAPTER THREE

> *If you are looking for actionable strategies to offset inflationary forces, jump to Chapter Six.*

> *"It is well enough that people of the nation do not understand our banking and monetary system, for if they did, I believe there would be a revolution before tomorrow morning."*
>
> **HENRY FORD**

> *"I would say [Fed policy] has been in some sense reverse Robinhood."*
>
> **KEVIN WARSH, FEDERAL RESERVE GOVERNOR 2006-2011**

The Federal Reserve Bank came into existence in 1913 and is the Central Bank for the United States. While independent, the Federal Reserve is ultimately accountable to the public and Congress, although many would question if the public has a say in this matter.

The Federal Reserve has almost unified control of the banking system and operates it as they desire. With the collapse of savings and loan banks in the '90s and the forced membership of national banks to the Federal Reserve system during the '80s, the only banks outside the realm of the Fed are credit unions, community banks, and industrial banks.

The Fed has enormous power and reach. It can move the nation with its words and actions. Its actions raise concern because, as economists believe, its actions led to the Great Depression by raising interest rates in 1928 and 1929 and cutting off the money supply and to the inflation of the '70s by increasing the money supply during the post-war period, which led to inflation in the '70s.

Could the Fed Be Driving Us into an Inflationary Spiral?

To begin our examination of the Fed's tools and techniques, a basic understanding of the Fed's structure is important. The Fed provides independent oversight of the banking system through its twelve member banks and the Federal Open Market Committee (FOMC). The FOMC comprises seven presidents of the banks and is led by the Chairman of the Federal Reserve, a position currently held by Jerome Powell. The FOMC examines economic data to determine its strategy based on its stated goal during its meetings.

Currently, the Fed's stated goal is to "promote the goals of maximum employment, stable price controls, and moderate long-term interest rates effectively." This stated objective has remained relatively consistent since 1977, when its stated goal was changed to address price instability (inflation).

Before 1977, the Federal Reserve's mandate attempted to adhere to the 1946 Employment Act, passed by Congress. The act declared that the federal government's policy was "to promote maximum employment, production and purchasing power."

With soldiers returning home from war, the nation desired to employ soldiers and maximize employment by creating monetary policies that drove business growth.

The policy mandate primarily focused on maintaining low-interest rates to finance growth and pay off the national debt incurred from the war. Interest rates were kept artificially low and reached levels we experience today by "monetizing" the debt.

That's a fancy word for the Fed placing U.S. Treasuries on its books instead of being offered to the general public where supply and demand determine the price and yield. By doing this, the money supply increases, and interest rates are suppressed.

Similarities to today abound. That is why we must understand the Federal Reserve's tools and techniques in order to understand the tsunami of inflation heading our way.

Having the power that they do, the Fed can either increase or decrease the money supply within the system to manipulate the economy. Sadly, their success rate is dismal and has led to the busts we've experienced countless times.

For a complete view of their financial bag of tricks, you can go to **https://www.federalreserve.gov/monetarypolicy/policytools.htm** to learn more or you can find it at **www.InflationBookResources.com** along with other resources and interviews I have with thought-leaders on inflation and what the future holds for your investments.

I'll stick with the primary tools they use to lay the groundwork for why inflation is rising and will continue to grow at a rampant rate.

Market Operations and Quantitative Easing

Since the mortgage meltdown, the Fed has engaged in a new strategy known as Quantitative Easing (QE). The Fed provides liquidity to the market by buying Treasuries or mortgage securities on the open market with money created out of thin air. In turn, the securities seller reinvests their proceeds somewhere in the system. They will either place the money in a bank or purchase another stock, bond, or asset.

By driving asset prices up with QE, the Fed makes investors feel wealthier as asset values increase. Evaluate your situation in recent years. You're probably happier seeing your investment account grow 30% or your home increase 25% in value! It's an aphrodisiac! Now compare that to how you feel when you lose 20%!

Increased "paper wealth" leads to more optimism which, in turn, drives the economy forward. As we discussed when evaluating inflation in Chapter Two, the psychology of economic participants plays a vital role in policies.

But here's the kicker. At one point in his career in 2002, presenting to the National Economics Club, former Fed Chairman Ben Bernanke said that the central bank could continually stoke inflation if needed, and that's exactly what they've done. As he eloquently noted,

> **INCREASED "PAPER WEALTH" LEADS TO MORE OPTIMISM WHICH, IN TURN, DRIVES THE ECONOMY FORWARD.**

"The U.S. government has a technology, called a printing press (or, today, its electronic equivalent), that allows it to produce as many U.S. dollars as it wishes at essentially no cost. By increasing the number of U.S. dollars in circulation, or even by credibly threatening to do so, the U.S. government can also reduce the value of a dollar in terms of goods and services, which is equivalent to raising the prices in dollars of those goods and services. We conclude that, under a paper-money system, a determined government can always generate higher spending and hence positive inflation."

While QE and its implementation were new, this concept had been around for years. John Maynard Keynes, the father of government spending, suggested filling bottles with money and burying them to stimulate the economy!

The idea was to have people dig up the money to get more money into their hands for spending. In those days, people still believed in working for money and were repulsed by free handouts. Today I'm not sure anyone would be willing to dig.

But Here's the Scary Part

Since the Covid pandemic began, the Fed's balance sheet has more than doubled, which had already been at a level unseen since its existence. As I write, the Fed purchases $120 billion of government bonds a month: $80 billion in Treasury debt and $40 billion in mortgage-backed securities. Mortgage-backed securities are created by mortgage lenders bundling loans and selling them to Fannie or Freddie Mac, who then sells them to investors.

Effectively, the Fed buys the assets and "suppresses" interest rates because they supply the demand for the purchase. If it weren't for the Fed, someone else would have to buy this government debt, and interest rates are purely a mixture of risk, term, the borrower, and the return expectations of the lender. With so much debt created by the government and business, interest rates should rise to entice purchasers, but they haven't because of the increase in the money supply.

With inflation hitting 7.9% and no sign of letting up, few rational investors would view a ten-year U.S. Treasury paying 1.78% as a good deal. In effect, that has a real interest rate of -6.12%!

We'll touch on this in later chapters because when US debt comes due the government issues new debt to pay off the old. Frankly, it's the biggest Ponzi scheme in operation by the definition of the term—using new money to pay off old investors. Federal prosecutors throw people in prison daily for running operations like this.

Naturally, the government plays by a different set of rules, but the consequences are the same. It's imperative you take action now to preserve your wealth.

The Fed's Balance Sheet Has Exploded Since 2004!

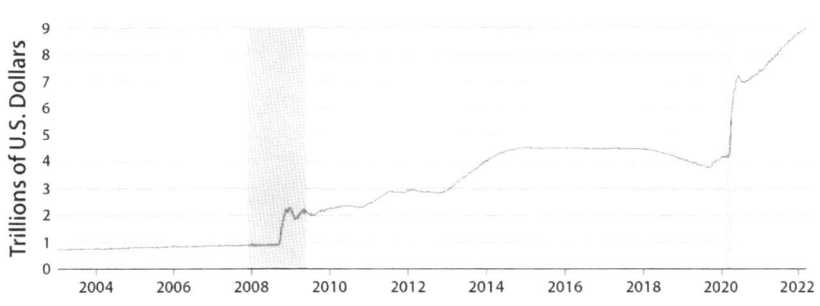

Source: Board of Governors of the Federal Reserve System (US)

This chart tells me serious inflationary waves are coming and coming quickly. Don't forget Bernanke's own words. Remember, his comments were in 2002 when the Fed's balance sheet was less than **$500 billion**.

"A determined government can always generate higher spending and hence positive inflation."

"A DETERMINED GOVERNMENT CAN ALWAYS GENERATE HIGHER SPENDING AND HENCE POSITIVE INFLATION."

Today, the Fed's balance sheet is $8.9 trillion. To understand how large that is, consider this. Germany's national debt is less than **$3 trillion**. Heavily indebted, Japan barely beats the Fed in size with $12 trillion. It's astounding to think about how much money they've pumped in the last 12 years.

It's also funny that the Fed's balance sheet was only $500 billion in 2002. Remember earlier that in 1968 the budget deficit swelled and brought screams of panic for what would be $200 billion today. Ponder and dwell on that for a moment.

Don't fall for the "This Time Is Different" mantra.

I must warn you, however, that you will hear very astute people and economists describe how "this time is different." They'll talk about the new dynamics of life and that we need not worry about the national debt, deficits, or the Fed's balance sheet. You'll even hear a fancy new term I mentioned earlier: Modern Monetary Theory.

Modern Monetary Theory: Spending Doesn't Matter

MMT became famous in 2019 as progressive Congresswoman Alexandria Ocasio-Cortez espoused the concept that spending and debt doesn't matter. It's a central concept of the Build Back Better proposal and the nearly $3.5 trillion proposed.

In a nutshell, under MMT, budget deficits and debt don't matter when a nation controls their currency because they have a printing press! Simply put, print as much as you want, and the Fed can place it on their books. For debt in circulation, print more to repay the money owed.

Sadly, this goes right back to what Milton Friedman had taught during the late '70s and '80s. Inflation is always the result of the printing press, which takes us right back to the experiment that began in 2008 by Federal Reserve Chairman Ben Bernanke.

As the Federal Reserve ramped up its purchases and began Quantitative Easing, the markets rose, and investors cheered.

Studying the correlation between QE and the markets, you'll notice that the market took a beating every time the Fed pulled back or even announced the idea of pulling back. The same will happen as the Fed eventually raises rates and decreases open market purchases, and we're seeing it right now as I write.

Look at what happened when they stopped open market purchases in 2015. The market dropped and suffered a tumultuous two years. Pay particular attention to the trend line directly in line with QE money flowing into the market.

As QE went, so went the market. The trend broke in 2017 as the market surged after the election and the regulatory reform of the Trump Administration. Still, as soon as a "reduction" of holdings by the Fed began in 2018, the market reacted and even ended down for 2018.

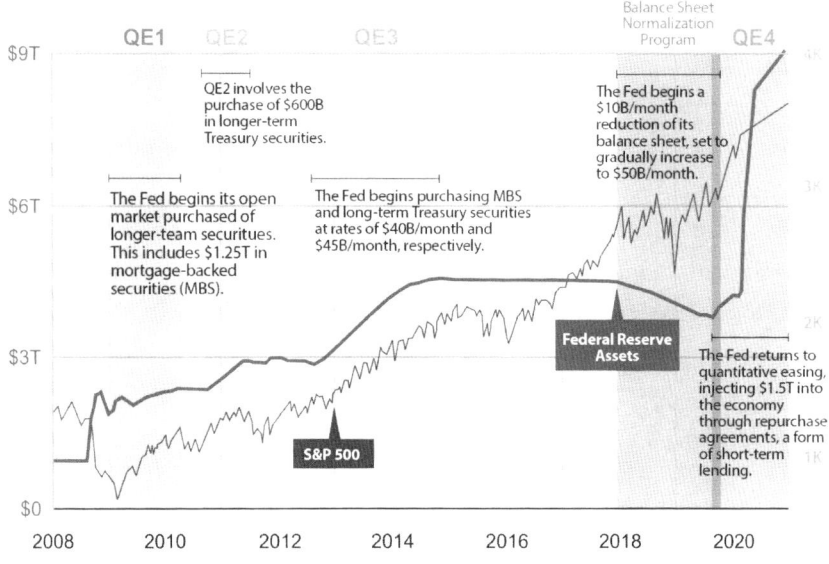

Source: Federal Reserve, CNBC

The entire concept of Quantitative Easing, though, is new and uncharted, and it's a big experiment never before attempted. Undoubtedly, it has successfully blunted interest rate increases because most asset purchases have been government debt.

But that's only created an environment where the government hasn't had to pay the actual cost for debt, so it has encouraged more! Remember, whatever you incentivize gets rewarded. Without the pain of interest on the debt, politicians could freely spend and soak the economy with promises in order to win votes.

Look no further than the $5.7 trillion spent since the Covid pandemic began! Worse yet, it has created a bubble that will eventually pop and destroy the lives of those unprepared.

As Milton Friedman would say when the economy grows on a sugar high or alcohol, correction involves pain, and pain is not something we're accustomed to. The governments only option is to kick the can down the road by engaging in the same tactics and inflating the money supply even further. It's this kicking of the can that leads to hyperinflation.

Reserve Requirements for Banks

Another strategy of the Fed to stimulate or strangle the economy is the reserve requirement for banks. Under our fractional banking system, money added becomes amplified by the reserve rate.

If the Fed requires a 10% reserve, when $1000 goes into the bank, the bank must hold $100 on hand. The other $900 is lent out to borrowers, which goes to another bank, which holds out $90 and lends out $810. Another bank receives the $810 and holds $81 and lends out the rest, and so on. By the fifteenth transaction in this example, the original $1,000 has become $7,930 into the economy and $794 in reserves at banks. Now, take it a step further.

If the Fed wants to increase the money supply, they lower the reserve requirement. To slow the growth of money, they raise the reserve requirement.

On March 26, 2020, the Federal Reserve lowered the requirement to ZERO, and it's remained there since! Even with inflation shooting through the roof, the reserve requirement as of January 2022 remains unchanged!

The Federal Funds Rate

The final strategy is the Federal Reserve funds rate. The funds rate is the interest rate charged to banks when accessing the Fed's discount window for money and is set by the Federal Open Market Committee (FOMC). This tool is the most prominent psychological technique used by the Fed to control the economy. The markets hold their breath until the monthly FOMC meeting transcript is released to know what will happen with the funds rate.

The simple talk of the Fed Chair discussing raising interest rates sends the markets in a tizzy because it means a higher cost of funds. In principle, banks go to the Fed for excess money to have on hand to meet reserve requirements if they've lent everything out or to push off their loans onto the Fed to free up cash on their books. Historically, this rate has averaged approximately 5.74%. Keep that number in your mind.

Go back to 2001 and the Dot-com crash and terrorist attacks. The Fed dropped the funds rate from 6.62% in November 2000 to 1.52% by December 2001. Since that time, we've become "trained" to believe interest rates should be low, but it wasn't that long ago when we found the rate at the historical average of 5.74%.

Every time we reach a new crisis situation, the Fed rewrites the rulebook and takes it even lower. The next stop will be negative interest rates! Of course, the European Central Bank has already blazed that trail!

In March 2020 the Fed lowered the funds rate to ZERO, and it's currently at 0.08% with an upper-level target of 0.25%!

The chart below of the funds rate reveals the downward trend we've experienced in rates since the '80s.

CHAPTER THREE: MONETARY POLICY & TECHNIQUES OF THE FED

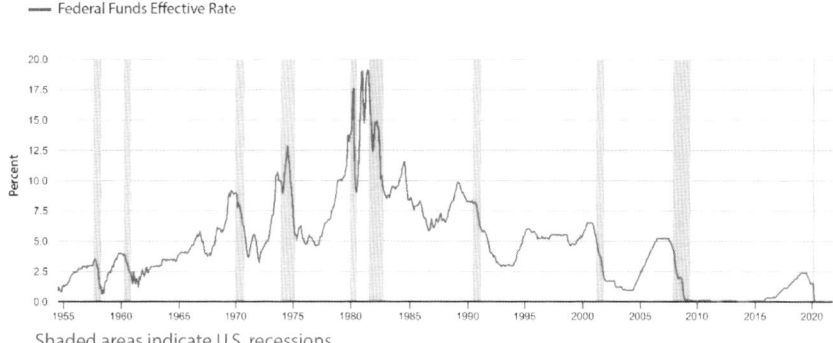

Shaded areas indicate U.S. recessions.

Source: Board of Governors of the Federal Reserve System (US)

Remember when the Fed raised rates in 2018?

It's important to recall from our mental history that in fall 2018, President Trump and Chairman Powell were the headlines of every news cycle. President Trump blasted Chairman Powell, whom he had appointed, because interest rates were raised to pump the brakes on the booming economy. With the economy growing and breaking previously set records for unemployment dating back to the '60s, inflation was low at 2.4%, and the GDP grew at 3%. The Fed moved to cool things down before it got too hot.

I can't say it enough, the funds rate is a major psychological tool, but it also acts to pump or siphon money in or out of the economy. As soon as they raised rates just a tiny bit, the economy and markets began to shudder.

According to news sources, Trump became enraged. He even contemplated firing Chairman Powell, whom he saw as driving the economy into recession. Powell had raised the funds rate to 2.5% from the lows in December 2016 of 0.50% through incremental steps. Every step of the way, the markets reacted negatively.

If you're invested in the stock market, remember, rising interest rates cause market upheaval! Plus, we have a gigantic asset bubble caused by the pumping of money by both the Fed and the federal government.

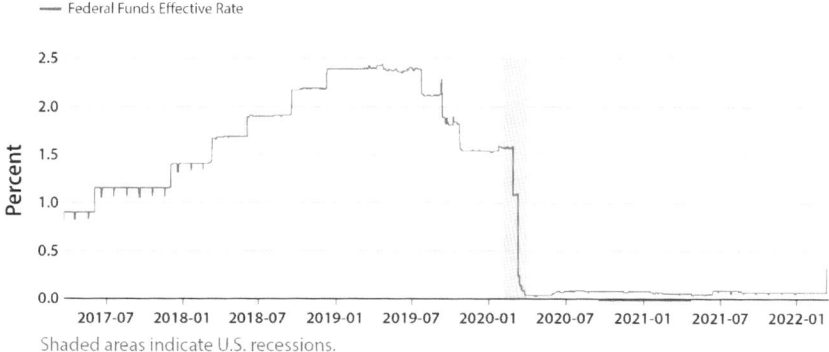

Source: Board of Governors of the Federal Reserve System (US)

As the funds rate ticked up, the markets reacted to the multi-step increase by shedding over 9% of their value. The S&P 500 finished December down 9.3%, establishing it as the 11th worst month for the index in the past half-century, and ended down for 2018.

Source: Yahoo Finance

In Chapter Five, we'll look at today's events. You'll find that January 2022 was one of the worst months for the market with the Russell 2000 down nearly 20% from its high in November and the S&P 500 down almost 5%. This was all before the market tumble which occurred as Russia invaded Ukraine in February.

Did the Fed raise interest rates? No. Just the talk and hint of rates having to go up faster than expected due to inflation sent shockwaves through the market in January of 2022.

The Prime Lending Rate & Borrowing

Another critical area of monetary policy is the prime lending rate. For clarification, the "prime rate" is the interest rate borrowers pay for loans, provided they have perfect credit. That rate is 3% higher than the upper limit of the funds rate.

Currently, the prime rate sits at 3.25%, down from highs of 5.5% in 2018 and 7.75% in September of 2007. We're living in a genuinely irrational time with meager interest rates, which means more money into the economy, which will continue to show itself in the inflation numbers we'll witness.

Why Isn't the Fed Addressing Inflation?

Why is the Federal Reserve maintaining low-interest rates with the economy running at full employment? (Anything under 4% is considered full employment.) This isn't a new phenomenon. You've also seen from the charts above that the Fed wasn't cutting back on its open market purchases of bonds. What is going on? Why are they doing what they're doing?

We have the lowest rates, massive pumping by the Fed, no reserve requirements, and all of this mixed in with horrific levels of government spending. Why are they not raising rates dramatically to slow the money supply?

It's kind of like when a bear has you trapped in a corner. What's the best route of escape? Stay, scream, punch, run, or act dead? None of the options are good.

But once again, I'll remind you, opportunities are always present. I'll show you why and how you can protect yourself from the silent killer of retirement in Chapter Six.

If you already understand the history of the '70s and agree we're entering a similar stage, you may want to fast forward to page 85. For the rest of you, let's look at why inflation raged in the late '60s to early '80s and what it did to the economy and the American psyche.

Visit **www.InflationBookResources.com** to access additional information and resources. There are interviews with thought-leaders on inflation, investments, the future, and much more. It's free of charge and my gift to you for investing in your future!

CHAPTER FOUR

IT'S BEGINNING TO LOOK A LOT LIKE THE '70s

> *If you are looking for actionable strategies to offset inflationary forces, jump to Chapter Six.*

"Domestic inflation reflects domestic monetary policy."
MARTIN FELDSTEIN
FORMER CHAIRMAN OF COUNCIL OF ECONOMIC ADVISORS

"In the absence of the gold standard, there is no way to protect savings from confiscation through inflation."
ALAN GREENSPAN
FEDERAL RESERVE CHAIRMAN 1987–2006

Many nations battled inflation after World War II as the economies adjusted from wartime production and pent-up consumer spending at home. The U.S. faced 18.1% inflation in 1946, followed by 8.8% in 1947. Many politicians in 2022 point to the late '40s as relevant to today's rip-roaring inflation. They identify a similar increased demand for products when soldiers returned home but fail to acknowledge the difference that the government then wasn't pumping massive amounts of money into the system after the war.

The difference between then and now is that the government rapidly decreased spending after World War II. Today's politicians also fail to mention that the economy faced a negative GDP in the post-war years of 1946–47. Darn those facts!

In fact, the economy shrunk 11.6% in 1946! That's vastly different from today, with the economy having grown at 5.7% since reopening from the Covid pandemic, one of the most robust GDP numbers since 1984.

Government Spending on the War & The Great Society

The most accurate comparison to today comes by way of the '60s to '80s. In 1960, John F. Kennedy faced a slumping economy and proceeded to push for the most significant tax cut to stimulate the economy. His goal was to lower the top marginal tax bracket from 90 to 70%.

JFK pushed his plan, saying, "Lower rates of taxation will stimulate economic activity and so raise the levels of personal and corporate income as to yield within a few years an increased—not a reduced—flow of revenues to the federal government."

This substantial tax law change passed in February of 1964 and was signed by his successor Lyndon Baines Johnson "LBJ" after JFK's assassination. What followed would live with us for many years to come.

LBJ pushed through a package of spending programs, known as The Great Society Programs, and later the Medicare and Medicaid Act in 1965. This substantial ramp-up in domestic spending coupled with tax cuts came in addition to the escalation of conflict in Vietnam.

With the increased spending, then Fed Chairman William McChesney Martin succumbed to pressure from LBJ to maintain low-interest rates to finance his spending spree.

Worse yet, as the Federal Reserve of St. Louis pointed out in an article from 2005 entitled, "President's Message: Volcker's handling of the great inflation taught us much," the Fed's lack of fortitude during this time gave the market the expectation that they would never deal with inflation. Inflation became ingrained in the market's thinking, and it was expected to occur!

CHAPTER FOUR: IT'S BEGINNING TO LOOK A LOT LIKE THE '70S

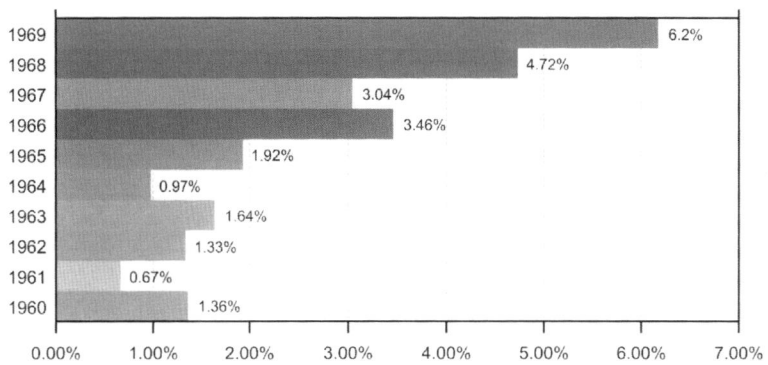

In 1968, Johnson raised taxes to offset expenditures, but the nation ran a historically high, non-wartime deficit of $25 billion. As I alluded to in Chapter One, $25 billion in deficit spending is equivalent to $199 billion in present-day dollars. Think about those numbers for a moment.

The worst part is that LBJ's spending packages still live with us and will continue to eat up more of the federal budget as baby boomers age and live longer lives.

As the nation continued deficit spending on the war and social programs, the annual inflation rate rose from the mid -1% ranges during the early '60s to 3%, then 4.7%, then nearly 6.2% in 1969.

> **INFLATION ALWAYS LAGS; IT'S NEVER IMMEDIATELY FELT BUT BUILDS IN THE SYSTEM.**

Once again, Milton Friedman's words that inflation is always a printing press problem rang true. But remember one key fact: Inflation always lags; it's never immediately felt but builds in the system.

That's one of the reasons why you shouldn't be fooled as time goes on and new reports come out about

www.InflationBook.com ■ 37

lowering inflation. As you'll see in our journey of the '70s, inflation fell many times, only to rise to new heights in the following years.

From LBJ to Nixon, Overspending Leads to Inflation

As is customary, once the government began spending, it never stopped. With the country facing economic issues, war, and social problems at home, Richard Nixon won by a landslide, promising to bring fiscal responsibility back to the White House in 1968, but he did precisely the opposite.

Instead, Nixon continued deficit spending, albeit with a few strange twists. The chart below reveals the budget deficits and the continual red ink during this period.

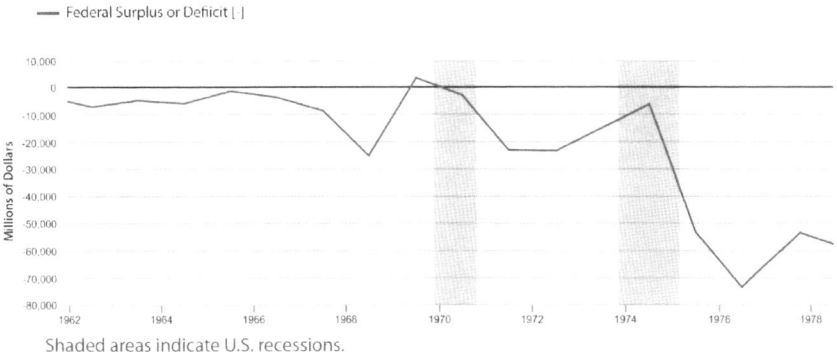

Shaded areas indicate U.S. recessions.

Source: Board of Governors of the Federal Reserve System (US)

While the economy had reached "full employment," averaging less than 4% every year since 1965, it created inflation on the cost-push side of the equation due to rising wages and deficit spending by the government coupled with low-interest rates created by the Fed.

Fed Chairman William Martin, who drew constant fire from Nixon, raised the funds rate from a low of 2.34% in 1964 to 9.38% in January of 1970 to stop inflation. That, in turn, led to the 1970 recession.

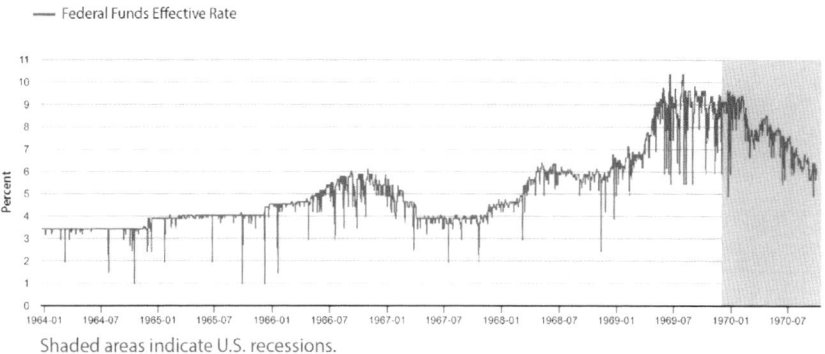

Shaded areas indicate U.S. recessions.

Source: Board of Governors of the Federal Reserve System (US)

Price Controls, Wage Freezes & the Death of the Gold Standard

As the public clamored for more to be done both to stop inflation and get the economy and stock market going, Nixon replaced Chairman Martin with Arthur Burns. Burns was a "yes man" for President Nixon and a proponent of easy money.

Burns proceeded to lower the funds rate from 9.38% in February of 1970 to 3% by the end of the year. Once again, the Fed used its tools to increase monetary supply to grow the economy, and in turn, inflation raged.

With inflation decimating incomes and wealth, the public then clamored for price controls and wage freezes, believing labor unions and greedy businessmen were responsible for the inflation they were facing. Sadly, the public tends to have very little idea of what's happening, and groupthink can lead to policies that have the opposite effect of the desired result. We call these unintended consequences.

At first, Nixon fought back against the idea of price controls. In 1970, Nixon even announced he would not institute price controls or wage freezes because doing so would harm the economy. Like with any good politician, however, views held one day are easily replaced when facing an election.

On August 15, 1971, Nixon addressed the nation to announce, "Today, I am ordering a freeze on all prices and wages throughout the United States." After a 90-day freeze, a Pay Board and Price Commission would have to approve all proposed changes.

Along with price and wage controls, Nixon also removed the United States from the gold standard, paving the way for unlimited spending and debt. I love the newspaper headline: **"Controlled Inflation."**

Photo Credit: The New York Times Archive

This decision was the culmination of the U.S. running a deficit in seven of the previous ten years, in fairness to Nixon, and the gold on hand at Fort Knox dwindled to a point about which *Time* magazine wrote on August 30th, 1971:

"Foreigners held three times as many dollars as the U.S. was capable of redeeming in gold, and they were demanding more and more gold because they were losing confidence in the U.S.'s will or ability to whip its economy in order."

Another point to ponder is that foreign nations hold over 20% of our debt. What happens if they lose confidence in the dollar? What types of problems exist if they lose faith in the dollar and stop purchasing U.S. debt?

With thirty trillion dollars of debt costing the government around 1% due to the low-interest rates, what will happen if rates were to rise to a level of 6% like we last saw in 2000?

This is the nightmare scenario that keeps the Fed up at night and why they've added debt to their books—to suppress interest rates.

The Tax Burden Nearly Doubles!

With the gold standard eliminated and an easy money Fed chairman, the '70s became a spending frenzy at every level of government. Nixon, who had run as a conservative and free-market believer, had succumbed to public pressure and political power.

But the actions intended to minimize pain only caused more pain. Controlling prices diminishes supply and leads to shortages as producers see no value or reward in producing more.

That's why price controls never work, but politicians love it because it seems like they're trying to do something! As Daniel Yergin and Joseph Stanislaw wrote in *The Commanding Heights: The Battle for the World Economy*, it was obvious that price controls didn't work:

> "Ranchers stopped shipping their cattle to the market, farmers drowned their chickens, and consumers emptied the shelves of supermarkets."

While struggling with prices and wages, state and local governments began overspending, leading to higher taxes. *Time* magazine wrote in March 1972 that, even as the tax burden on the federal level had lowered, local and state governments replaced them with their own!

Citizens faced increased state income taxes, sales taxes, property taxes, and sin taxes on tobacco and alcohol. Real estate values had boomed at the local level due to inflation, and with it, real estate taxes.

That's one of the reasons why real estate is the best hedge against inflation because as inflation grows the price of the asset increases along with the rents charged! More on that later in Chapter Six.

Overall, the tax burden for individuals nearly doubled between 1960 and 1970, from $711 to $1,348, and it led to a hit new song—"The Tax Man" by the Beatles!

War and Oil Embargo

On the world stage, on October 6th, 1973, war broke out in the Middle East, just as it had in 1967. During the Jewish holiday of Yom Kippur, Arab forces mostly from Egypt, Syria, and Jordan launched an invasion of Israel. While the United States and the U.S.S.R. inched closer to war, the Arab nations instituted an oil embargo of Israel's allies, which included the U.S.

Thanks to Nixon's price controls in 1971, domestic oil producers had been driven out of business or scaled back production and were replaced by lower-cost oil from the Middle East. Then that low-cost oil from the Middle East was cut off.

Shown in the chart below, energy production in the U.S. grew to keep up with demand; however, you can see the line flattening 1971 with the price controls.

CHAPTER FOUR: IT'S BEGINNING TO LOOK A LOT LIKE THE '70S

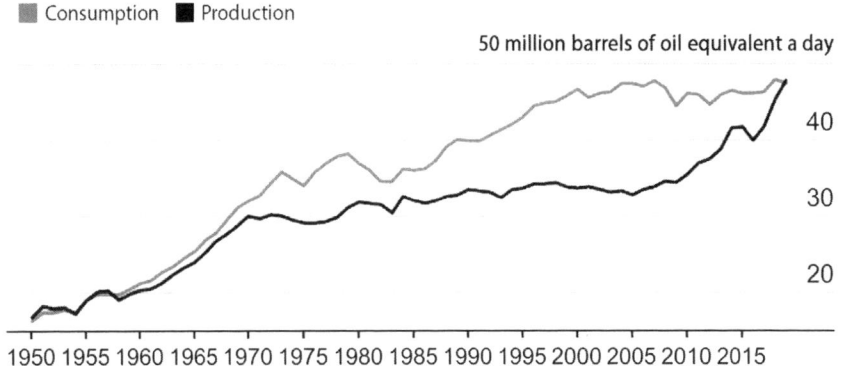

Source: U.S. Energy Information Administration

It's a lesson to study and learn from.

Since the fracking revolution which began in the late 2000s, coupled with President Trump's opening of federal lands and limiting regulation, the United States became a "net exporter" of energy in 2020. We had finally reached energy independence!

In fact, fracking created so much natural gas that the laws had to be updated since the Jones Act, passed in 1975, prohibited selling energy outside of the United States. With energy flowing in the U.S., there became a glut of energy, which drove down prices (supply and demand). Eventually, the Jones Act was repealed, and the United States once again began exporting energy.

> **SOMEHOW GOVERNMENT STATISTICIANS BELIEVE WE CAN LIVE WITHOUT ENERGY AND FOOD!**

Energy independence is essential because energy is the main driver of inflation along with food prices. Be careful when you hear "core inflation" because it's a deceptive number that excludes food and energy from the inflation number. *Somehow government statisticians believe we can live without energy and food!*

As I mentioned in earlier chapters, it's upsetting that since President Biden was elected, his actions and policies have attacked the oil and gas industry instead of encouraging it.

The result? Fuel costs have risen nearly 60% in the last year because supply hasn't kept up with demand. We've even had to "beg" the Saudis to pump more oil because our producers can't produce enough! And that was prior to the Russian invasion of Ukraine! But to understand how important energy is for an economy, let's go back to the '70s.

Gas Lines, Energy Shortages, and Stock Market Collapse

In 1973, the nation imported nearly 6.2 million barrels a day to meet demand. Naturally, the OPEC embargo sent shock waves through the nation, and the stock market plunged. In 1973, the Dow Jones Industrial Average dropped -16.58%, then in 1974 it fell -27.57%. In the meantime, inflation skyrocketed to 6.16% in '73 and then 11.03% in 1974.

On April 8th, 1974, *Time* magazine wrote, "In the twelve months ended in February, prices in the U.S. climbed 10%, and in the month, they were springing up at a compounded annual rate of more than 16%."

Then came the calls for energy conservation. There were calls to lower the highway speed limit, raise fuel use and electricity taxes, and cut back on outdoor lighting. The nation went into energy shock, and overnight, America's love affair with big power cars was over!

In 2021, Americans recently experienced gas lines and supply shocks, which brought flashbacks to the '70s. Hackers took control of the Colonial Pipeline, and people on the east coast experienced fuel shortages and limited supplies. Another example occurred after hurricane Katrina when oil prices leaped. Many forget, but this price and supply jolt was the beginning of the end of the real estate boom.

The point is that we need to keep an eye on global events because they can disrupt supply chains and supercharge inflation. When we were producing our own oil and fulfilling our needs, foreign events like those in Libya or the Middle East didn't affect things. Now they will.

Update March 15th: Ukrainian War

With the outbreak of war in Ukraine, much of what I had written prior to that event has come to pass. As the world has unified to support Ukraine and punish Russia, oil prices shot up to the highest level since 2008. Today, oil reached $130 a barrel, and some are predicting $300 a barrel later this year. Still, there has been no action by our government to expand and encourage more exploration in the United States. In fact, our leaders are considering purchasing oil from Iran or Venezuela.

AAA reported the average cost per gallon for unleaded gas was $4.06 compared to $2.76 one-year prior—an increase of 47%! Sorry, that was yesterday. Today, gas prices jumped over .30 cents a gallon and the national average is now $4.36. In turn, economists are warning of an economic recession as the average household is being hit with an additional $2,500 of fuel costs a year.

This is why energy independence for any nation is crucial for prosperity.

But it's not only energy costs. Food prices are set to skyrocket as diesel fuel has increased and the world's wheat supply could be

> **THIS IS WHY ENERGY INDEPENDENCE FOR ANY NATION IS CRUCIAL FOR PROSPERITY.**

severely impacted. Ukraine has forever been known as "the breadbasket of Europe." Supplying nearly 25% of the world's corn and ⅓ of the world's wheat, if production is impacted in the Ukraine, the laws of supply and demand will take hold. Prices will rise drastically and there are warnings of food shortages.

I see so much of what I'm writing taking place before my eyes. In my earlier manuscripts, I wrote about the potential for war and what it would mean for energy costs. Now, I'll direct you to what really concerns me.

As the U.S. levies sanctions on Russia, that will be a catalyst for Russia to develop a closer relationship with China. The only reason sanctions hurt a nation is because everything in the world is based on the U.S. Dollar. We're the world's reserve currency and China knows this. I'm not worried about Russia, even though they are a nuclear power. My concern is China. Recently my feelings were confirmed when I heard an interview with former National Security Advisor, Lt. General H.R. McMaster on the Joe Rogan Podcast (Episode 1763).

I encourage you to listen to it and I have linked the interview at **www.InflationBookResources.com**.

Thanks to the wise guys in government who decided to allow a state controlled economy into the World Trade Organization in 2001, China has manipulated things to have a competitive advantage utilizing low-cost labor. In many cases, forced slave labor. Today, they're an economic powerhouse, right behind the United States.

China, of course, is growing economically and militarily. They're expanding throughout the world with their Belt and Road Program and using the wealth we've created for them by purchasing their goods to become a global adversary. Plus, they've done a nice job of stealing our technology and factory jobs.

With Russia's energy, China could move to eliminate the dollar as the world's reserve currency, especially as China's influence grows and countries look to hitch a ride with them. Imagine how that could rapidly change the picture! God help us if this occurs.

Continue to keep an eye on global markets for energy and food. It will tell you where things are headed but let's return to our journey in time and the disastrous policies of Gerald Ford.

President Ford's Fight with Inflation: Pump & Tax

On August 8th, 1974, President Nixon resigned due to the Watergate scandal, and Gerald Ford took over. To combat inflation and the unemployment rate that had jumped from 4.9% in 1973 to 7.2% in 1974, President Ford planned a three-stage operation which sounds eerily similar to plans used today.

The plan called for a quick infusion of $16 billion via rebates on taxes (approximately $90 billion in current value) to stimulate spending followed by a new "energy tax" to generate $30 billion, which would be recycled back into the economy through tax cuts. It sounds like a Green Energy Tax, which was touted recently.

Sound familiar? Stimulating the economy with stimulus checks coupled with new taxes on other sectors of the economy, primarily oil and gas, to fund an expanded child tax credit and other social programs? History seems to be repeating in an eerily similar fashion.

Another amusing part of President Ford's plan to fight inflation was his "WIN" campaign—Whip Inflation Now! With "WIN" campaign buttons, coffee cups, and signs (that really sticks it to inflation!), President Ford asked the public not to purchase anything unless absolutely necessary or medically needed.

Have you ever noticed, every time the government creates a problem, they come up with ridiculous ideas to combat the problem such as campaign buttons or driving 55 on the highway?

Economic Migraine, Pain, and Bloody Stock Market

It's safe to say the '70s were painful. The economy was in disarray with rising interest rates, inflation, and stock market losses. The tax burden expanded, coupled with utter frustration and fear in the American psyche. *Time* magazine in 1974 summed it up best in an article entitled, "Seeking Relief from a Massive Migraine:"

"The U.S. is afflicted by a massive economic migraine, and more than 200 million Americans know too well just how much it hurts. Their incomes, savings, and lifestyles are being assailed by a whole group of aches and pains. There is feverish inflation, constriction of credit, and throbbingly high-interest rates. The stock market has scarcely been so shaky since 1929. Just about everybody who buys, sells, borrows, or invests has that overall feeling of unease. And there is no fast relief in sight."

Throughout the '70s, a buildup of government spending that began with LBJ's Great Society programs and the Vietnam War and continued with Nixon's policies of price controls and fiat money and was topped off by Ford's rebates and energy taxes caused inflation to leap. Once again, I can't say it enough: inflation lags.

Unemployment rose to 8.25% in 1975 during the recession, and it would remain persistently high throughout the late '70s and early '80s, giving rise to a new term: **Stagflation!**

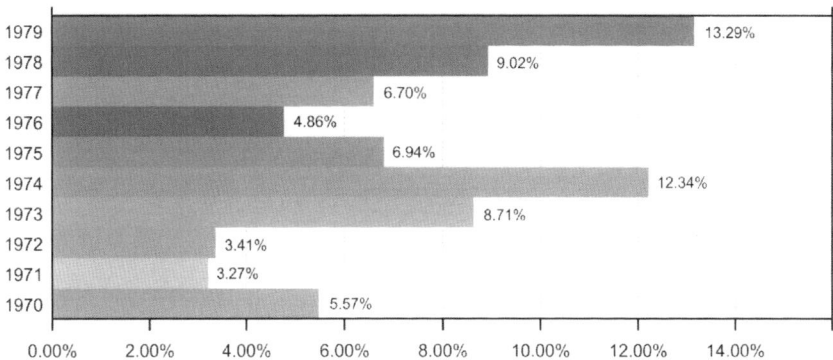

Carter Gets Tough with Inflation: Take the Pain

In 1977 President Carter took office with an economy that had expanded in 1976 at 5.4% after the recession of '74 and '75; however, inflation remained consistently high as the Fed lowered rates and the government continued overspending, thereby increasing the money supply.

To his credit, Carter wasn't a politically expedient leader because he could have done whatever he wanted. Riding high with a 72% approval rating and his party controlling both houses of Congress, he quickly could have passed and implemented his national health insurance plan, which he campaigned on.

Instead, Carter turned out to be far more cautious in his economic policy than previous presidents, as he sought to attack inflation and energy. Compare that to today.

With razor-thin margins in both houses of Congress, President Biden passed a $1.9 trillion Covid relief bill in March 2021 and a $1.2 trillion infrastructure bill in October and is pushing hard for his $3.5 trillion Build Back Better plan.

Following the advice of Federal Reserve Chairman William Miller, President Carter slowed government spending and even backed away from his proposal to give every American a rebate check of $50 ($250 in 2021 dollars) to stimulate growth, fearing it would add to the inflationary fire.

Miller told Carter what Milton Friedman had preached.

"If the government would stop feeding inflation by running big deficits, we can look forward to a model economy five, six, seven years from now."

Finally, the Fed was prepared to get serious, and it seemed the government was also ready to join the fight.

Understanding the importance of energy, President Carter proposed an ambitious national energy policy. Unfortunately, his approaches failed to produce results and even backfired. One such strategy was to maintain price controls on oil and gas.

Price and wage controls initiated under Nixon had ended in 1973; however, the oil and gas industry remained under a price control system. Carter proposed a higher price ceiling but not high enough to incentivize new drilling.

Consequently, oil supply from American fields remained constrained, and the supply situation only added to what occurred in 1978 with the overthrow of the Shah of Iran.

Following the Iranian Revolution, the loss of nearly 7% of the world's oil sent energy prices soaring and caused the return of gas lines throughout America. Once again, inflation topped 9% in '78 and 13.3% in '79.

CHAPTER FOUR: IT'S BEGINNING TO LOOK A LOT LIKE THE '70S

Meanwhile, Carter and Miller engaged in an economic dance no one wants to face, and it's a dance the United States will face in 2022.

A surging economy from '76 to'78 with unemployment averaging 6% and excess dollars in the system drove up asset prices and spending, which in turn drove inflation. In response, the President and the Fed announced dramatic actions to tackle the spiraling situation and produce a "soft landing."

First, the Fed raised the funds rate to 9.5%, the sharpest jump in 45 years, and reduced available funds for the banks. The economy reacted and crashed from its sugar high of easy money into a recession with higher interest rates and less money in the system.

Yet again, the strategy of a soft landing failed. Keep that in mind when you hear the Fed and government talk of a soft landing and remember the words from economist Otto Eckstein in 1979:

"There is not a single instance of success in raising interest rates to moderate the economy without creating a major disturbance. The Federal Reserve has carried the policy too far every single time."

Carter Confronts the Nation and the Crisis of Confidence

As the nation struggled with increasing unemployment, high inflation, low wage growth, and a faltering economy and stock market, President Carter took to the airwaves on July 15th, 1979, for his infamous "Malaise Speech."

Scholars rank this speech as the most depressing presidential address of all time. You can find a link to the speech at **www.InflationBook Resources.com**. Similarities in attitudes between then and now abound. In fact, it's scary to see how much things have changed but they're still the same!

King Solomon's words from Ecclesiastes once again ring true. There is nothing new under the sun.

President Carter began his speech by identifying the issues facing the Nation.

"As you know, there is a growing disrespect for government and churches and schools, the news media, and other institutions. This is not a message of happiness or reassurance, but it is the truth and a warning. We remember when the phrase "sound as a dollar" was an expression of absolute dependability until ten years of inflation began to shrink our dollar and our savings. We believed that our Nation's resources were limitless until 1973 when we had to face a growing dependence on foreign oil."

Carter laid out his strategy for energy independence and even cheered on coal for energy freedom. Looking back at history, I am amazed how people can forget. Today, progressive Liberals want to eliminate coal and put shackles around the American economy by limiting the use of natural resources we have readily available, yet President Carter knew it was what the country needed for energy independence and freedom!

President Carter went on to outline how this war on Energy would be won.

"Point four: I'm asking Congress to mandate, to require as a matter of law, that our Nation's utility companies cut their massive use of oil by fifty percent within the next decade and switch to other fuels, especially coal, our most abundant energy source. We will protect our environment. But when this Nation critically needs a refinery or a pipeline, we will build it. You know we can do it. We have natural resources. We have more oil in our shale alone than several Saudi Arabia's. We have more coal than any nation on earth."

As the '70s came to a close, "stagflation" was the most used word in the nation. Coined by Washington Post columnist Joseph Kraft, stagflation was everything the country had experienced during the decade. High inflation, high unemployment, an energy crisis, a declining dollar, increased government spending, and jobs going overseas because deindustrialization had ripped the nation apart.

What took $100 to purchase in 1969 would cost $262.94 by 1982. During Carter's presidency, inflation rose 6.7% in 1977, 9% in '78, 13% in '79, and 12.5% in '80. Could it get any worse? Sadly, it could.

High-Interest Rates Squash Inflation and Kill the Economy (1979–1981)

With the economy spiraling out of control, President Carter appointed Paul Volcker to become the Fed Chairman in August 1979. Volcker began to implement draconian policies to rein in the rampant inflation, including reversing many of the cheap and easy money policies.

In a shocking move, Volcker jumped prime lending rates from 12.25% to 19.50% in only six months!

As he so eloquently said while chomping on his cigar, "The greatest risk beyond doubt facing the economy is accelerating inflation. Not only do rapid price rises bring direct pain and distortions, but they also prepare the way for a serious recession."

In essence, Volcker's strategy was simple. Deprive inflation of its fuel—money. The Fed's policy shifted to target the money supply and maintain price stability.

With prices running away, economic recession, and inflation jumping, President Carter was pummeled in the 1980 election by Ronald Reagan. Inflation had now consumed four American presidents.

The Reagan Revolution Begins

President Reagan was determined to return the government to its size before LBJ's social programs were established and cast his vision of a new path of fiscal restraint, budget cuts to government, and lifting of onerous tax constraints hobbling the economy. He also sought to end the stagflation nightmare the country had endured.

During the election year, unemployment had reached 7.2%, and inflation continued at a torrent pace of 12.52%.

In 1981, Volcker had cut rates to get the economy out of recession, lowering the prime rate from 20% in January 1981 to 15.75% in December, and the economy responded growing 2.5%. But inflation remained stubbornly high at 8.92%, with unemployment increasing to 8.5%.

Joseph Pechman, Director of Brookings Institute, commented, "Reagan may find that inflation has run away from him before he even gets started on his plans."

With a divided Congress, President Reagan passed a sweeping tax reduction that saw the top tax bracket drop from 70% to 50%, along with deep budget cuts in non-military areas of government.

While Volcker opposed increased military expenditures, Reagan's economic team argued it wouldn't promote inflation. Their action to cut other budget areas would signal that an era of small government was finally here. Economists point to this action as the one which showed that the government was as committed to fighting inflation as the Fed.

The problem was that the economy still suffered from stagflation—high interest rates, high unemployment, and high inflation. It seemed inflation was entrenched in the United States economy and mind.

As *Time* magazine wrote on March 8th, 1982, "Worst of all. America's money miseries have become the ghoulish flipside to the Good Life. For cash-squeezed consumers by the millions, shopping on credit for everything from a new suit of clothing to cars, kitchen appliances, even a roof over one's head, is increasingly painful. Indeed, by the common consent of economists, towering interest rates have done more than any other single factor to drive the U.S. into a recession that still threatens to push unemployment to a post-World War II high."

The Public Call for Volcker's Head!

As the economy shrank -1.8% and unemployment soared to 10.8% in 1982, Volcker stuck to his guns and kept rates at 15.75%, only to slowly drop them to 11.50% by the end of the year.

While the public cried for Volcker's firing and his head on a platter, Reagan remained neutral, understanding government roles and the Fed's position of power. President Reagan, to his credit, supported Volcker, understanding that price stability was imperative. It also ushered in a new era of the Federal Reserve with a focus on maintaining price stability which has served us since.

President Reagan and Volcker understood that while their actions were unpopular, they were vital to break the back of inflation.

Do we have leaders like that today? To eradicate inflation, do we have anyone who will step up the way they did in the early '80s? Even as I write, St. Louis Federal Reserve President Jim Bullard has called for rapid interest rate increases even before the next FOMC meeting to contain inflation while others are still maintaining that inflation is short-lived.

> **DO WE HAVE LEADERS LIKE THAT TODAY? TO ERADICATE INFLATION, DO WE HAVE ANYONE WHO WILL STEP UP THE WAY THEY DID IN THE EARLY '80s?**

A Return to Normalcy!

Following the brutally high interest rates and high unemployment of the early 1980s, inflation finally moderated in 1982. Meanwhile, the economy took off with the tax cuts and optimism of a bright American future. GDP boomed 4.6% in 1983, 7.2% in '84, and 4.2% in '85. In 1984, President Reagan was re-elected in a landslide, taking every state except Minnesota. Reagan's television ads best summed up the country's mood and feeling: "It's Morning in America Again."

By 1986, the Fed had lowered the prime rate to 7.5%, and inflation remained moderate in the 3% range. Finally, it seemed, the awful years of inflation were a thing of the past.

One often overlooked change that helped break the back of inflation was the 1981 tax law change that adjusted the taxable income bracket to inflation beginning in 1985.

No longer could government increase taxes without voting for it.

Today, a few areas of the tax code are not indexed for inflation; however, during the '60s and '70s, nothing in the tax code was indexed! Inflationary growth propelled incomes and pushed taxpayers into higher tax brackets. This led to the new term: bracket creep.

For every 10% of inflation, income gains pushed individuals into the next tax bracket yielding an additional 5% to 6% of income tax! It was a built-in tax escalator—a politician's dream. It also led people to believe that the government wanted inflation to solve their budgetary woes.

Caveat emptor, however, because not every area of the income tax system is indexed for inflation. Remember the Alternative Minimum Tax or "AMT" as most people lovingly called it?

Created in 1969 to target 155 taxpayers earning over $200,000 a year (equivalent to $1.5 million today) and paying nothing in federal income taxes, by 2017, AMT trapped nearly 5.2 million taxpayers who paid almost $36 billion in federal taxes.

That is also why I'm highly suspicious of new taxes aimed at only a few because history shows that the few become the many! In the next chapter, I'll discuss other aspects of our tax code and provide proof for why, once again, inflation is being allowed to run rampant. Let me tell you, it's part of a plan.

What Happened to Stock Market Returns During Inflationary Times?

Beware! You will hear financial advisors and Wall Street saying that you must stay invested in the market to outpace inflation!

Nothing could be further from the truth.

Wall Street loves fantasy stories with half-truths. Total returns including dividends were 95.65% from 1969 to 1981. That's an annualized return of 5.3% per year.

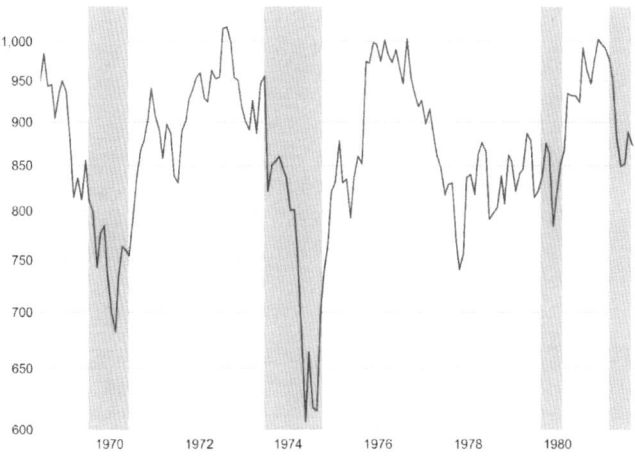

Source: Macrotrends.net

But here is the dirty secret Wall Street won't tell you.

After accounting for inflation, the *total return over that period was -21.01% or an annualized loss of -1.80%.* An investor in the stock market lost money every year during the last period of high inflation! That's provided they stayed invested during the tumultuous ups and downs of this period, but it gets worse.

Source: Macrotrends.net

Look at this chart of 1969 to 1981 and ask yourself whether you would have stayed invested if you watched your account thrashed on a monthly basis!

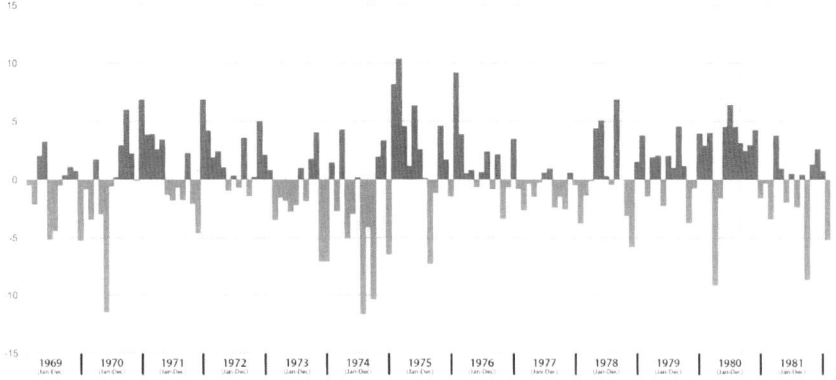

With our history lesson for a point of reference behind us, it's time to understand our current situation and who benefits and loses from inflation. The warning signs on the horizon are evident, and there's still time to act upon the strategies I share in Chapter Six.

Shift your mindset and realize that inflation isn't going away. Sure, there will be periods of relief, but long-term inflation is here to stay, just as we learned from the '70s.

Hopefully, we encounter someone like Paul Volcker who decisively stops inflation before it spirals out of control. Still, you'll learn how physical assets like real estate and other alternative investments will keep you one step ahead of the inflationary spiral.

Visit **www.InflationBookResources.com** to access additional information and resources. There are interviews with thought-leaders on inflation, investments, the future, and much more. It's free of charge and my gift to you for investing in your future!

CHAPTER FIVE

INFLATION ROARS BACK TO LIFE

> *If you are looking for actionable strategies to offset inflationary forces, jump to Chapter Six.*

"*Inflation has risen, largely reflecting transitory factors.*"
FEDERAL RESERVE APRIL 28, 2021, FOMC STATEMENT
https://www.federalreserve.gov/monetarypolicy/files/monetary20210428a1.pdf

"*I am ready to retire the word transitory . . . I can agree that that hasn't been an apt description of what we are dealing with.*"
TREASURY SECRETARY JANET YELLEN IN *THE NEW YORK TIMES*, DECEMBER 2, 2021

With Covid pandemic relief money flooding the economy, the government went further in March of 2021, passing the $1.9 trillion American Rescue Plan. It was a classic money pump of stimulus checks and money for state governments and any other group or organization to which the government could imagine giving money.

Worse yet, they laid the groundwork for Universal Income Benefit payments as Americans became addicted to monthly checks from the government for doing nothing!

The amount of expenditures and stimulus concerned Larry Summers, President Obama's economic advisor and Treasury Secretary under President Clinton. Summers appeared on various news outlets and even wrote an Op-Ed column in the Washington Post claiming it would spark an inflationary fire.

While leader after leader within the administration and the Fed tried to dismiss his claims, in the end he was correct. After nine months in 2021 of the White House and the Fed Chairman reading their talking points that inflation was only "transitory" and that it would soon recede, Fed Chairman Powell finally confessed they would retire that term in November of 2021.

In December, inflation hit 7% and 7.5% in January 2022. But as I've noted earlier, if the government were to use the same CPI index used in the early '80s we'd be over 15% inflation!

The Fed is Behind the Curve, and It Won't End Well

When the economic numbers for December 2021 hit the wires on January 7th, the market was mixed. However, former economic advisor to President Trump, Larry Kudlow, sounded the alarm. On Fox Business with host Neil Cavuto, Kudlow commented that the markets were reading the numbers wrong when they were disappointed with the jobs numbers.

As he told Cavuto, "The quit rate was 3%, the highest ever on record, meaning that people are moving up the pay scale to new jobs."

Kudlow went on to say that the average hourly earnings for workers had increased almost 10%, a massive uptick.

If you recall from earlier, the quit rate statistics came about in the 2000s by Fed Chairman Alan Greenspan to measure individuals leaving one job to move to another, presumably for higher pay.

As of February 2022, workers are in high demand, and higher wages lure the limited supply of willing participants. The Bureau of Labor reports there are 10.9 million unfilled jobs, while the demand for quality workers has led to a massive uptick in hourly wages of nearly 10%.

In our Freedom Founders Community, many of our dentists and professional practice owners on the east and west coasts experienced staffing issues early in 2021, and our members took that information to wall off their staff and stayed ahead of the curve by providing pay raises and flexible schedules. We call this "on-time information."

Not having on-time information is one of the reasons lone wolves get slaughtered.

With the business environment constantly changing and evolving, our goal should be to surround ourselves with others from whom we can learn and gather wisdom. What are they seeing? How are they overcoming challenges in their business?

The workforce participation situation is a real conundrum because we're missing four million working-class males between the ages of 25 and 54, who have dropped out of the labor force. I won't go into that many factors for this, but the lack of supply of workers, coupled with strong demand for labor, has sent wages skyrocketing, adding additional fuel to the inflationary fire.

The real gut punch.

On his show, Kudlow mentioned that Steve Mnuchin, the former Treasury Secretary under President Trump, had said that **the Fed was behind the curve on raising interest rates and slowing the inflationary spiral.**

"Why are rates still at rock bottom levels when inflation is shooting up, pay for workers is rapidly rising at levels not seen since the '70s, and the economy is at full employment?" Then Kudlow ended his interview with this:

> "WHY ARE RATES STILL AT ROCK BOTTOM LEVELS WHEN INFLATION IS SHOOTING UP, PAY FOR WORKERS IS RAPIDLY RISING AT LEVELS NOT SEEN SINCE THE '70s, AND THE ECONOMY IS AT FULL EMPLOYMENT?"

"Neil, I'm worried it may not end well. How many times in your career have you seen the Feds engineer a soft landing?"

But the question bears asking ourselves. Why is the Federal Reserve not taking action right now to cut off the fuel of easy money engulfing the economy?

The simple answer is that the government and its balance sheet benefit from higher than usual inflation. Politicians have made many promises. Plus, they're in a dangerous situation with few options.

Remember the Greenback Labor Party in the late 1800s discussed in Chapter One? They called for a return of the greenback to fiat status, unchained to gold, so the fiat money would inflate and, thus, reduce their debt.

Curiosity, Evaluation, and Examination are Vital for Success

When I was in dental school, observing and evaluating was the mantra of our studies. I've carried this approach into my daily life, observing and assessing various aspects of life and economics. This strategy has been beneficial in times of economic turbulence.

One recent case was when my mentor and the "Professor of Harsh Reality" Dan S. Kennedy and I sat around a table in the summer of 2020. We watched the forced strangulation of the economy and the destruction of small businesses coupled with the fanatical growth of local, state, and federal government in dictating every aspect of a person's life. We hypothesized and brainstormed what would happen next and began writing *Own Your Freedom* because we knew freedom was under attack.

As we expected, freedoms were curtailed, and individuals ran to the government for help. I don't fault anyone for taking PPP loans or cashing their stimulus checks, but handouts are never free.

What the government giveth, they'll take away in other ways like inflation or the future tax increases soon to come upon us.

The government pumped funds into the economy, and the Federal Reserve doubled the size of its balance sheet by over **$4.9 trillion**. Imagine, before the Covid pandemic, the federal government's budget was **$4.4 trillion**, and they were already spending with a deficit.

Since the Covid pandemic began in March 2020, the federal government has continued its bloated budget but has thrown in an additional $5.7 trillion of pandemic relief on top of $4.9 trillion by the Federal Reserve! These numbers are so large that we can't even wrap our heads around them.

And I haven't even thrown in the $1.2 trillion infrastructure bill passed in the fall of 2021, or the proposed Build Back Better plan they want to pass for $3.5 trillion. At this point, we're like Scrooge McDuck swimming around in a bathtub of money.

Like Milton Friedman said, easy money is like alcohol . . .

Easy money feels good initially, but too much of it causes problems. When the problems come, and there will be problems, taking the pain is too harsh, so it's masked over and kicked down the road.

Ask yourself this. If the country is hurting so badly from the pains of the Covid pandemic that the Fed needs to keep interest rates rock bottom and have zero reserve requirements for banks, why is the unemployment rate 3.5% with eleven million jobs unfilled?

Why are there four million people who have yet to return to work from the pre-pandemic months? How is it that everyone seems to be spending money like there's no tomorrow?

The economy seems to have done what President Trump predicted with a V-shaped bounce back as the economy was reopened with GDP growth of 5.7% in 2021. That's one of the most robust GDP numbers since 1984! However, still as of this publication, the Fed has not changed anything. Why?

The government flooded the market with money through stimulus checks, nearly a 100% increase in the child tax credit that became payable to households with children at the rate of $300 per month per child, and all sorts of other goodies. Remember the $600 per week unemployment relief payment early in the pandemic?

The expectancy of free and easy money has become part of our culture, and that is a terrible sign.

Worse yet, the markets and government are so addicted to easy money that even the talk of the Fed raising interest rates has sent shockwaves through the market.

We find ourselves in the most precarious position and a place we've never been before! I know I've told you this inflationary spike reminds other astute economists and me of the late '60s to early '80s, but the additional complications make it worse.

You've read and seen the headlines—Inflation running at its highest level since 1982! Monster federal government deficits. Companies unable to find workers driving up wages. Sign-on bonuses, incentives to work, low costs loans, and zero percent financing!

On the other hand, you've heard the ministry of propaganda telling us it's only transitory and will soon pass. I urge you to let history be your guide and evaluate the other factors at play.

Be curious and open to what's in store for us because that's where wealth is created or lost. I have a particular name for what is about to take place.

The Great Wealth Transfer

Right now, we're on the cusp of a historic wealth transfer as the easy money policies of the Fed slam into the changing dynamics of the world economies and demographics in the United States. Due to Social Security, Medicare, and Medicaid, those demographic changes are about to blow up our federal budget.

> **THE PEOPLE WHO ARE UNAWARE WILL BE DECIMATED, BUT THOSE WHO UNDERSTAND THE GAME CAN RUN FOR HIGHER GROUND.**

The people who are unaware will be decimated, but those who understand the game can run for higher ground.

While the national debt approaches $30 trillion, the actual unfunded obligations for Social Security, Medicare, and other promises have reached levels that are impossible to imagine. Some put the price tag at $77 trillion; others, like Truth in Accounting, place the figure near $120 trillion broken down in the chart below.

United States Government Financial Breakdown

What the Federal Government Has*	
Assets	$5.95 trillion
What the Federal Government Owes	
Medicare benefits	$55.12 trillion
Social Security promises	$41.20 trillion
Publicly held debt	$21.08 trillion
Military & civilian retirement benefits	$9.41 trillion
Other liabilities	$2.25 trillion
Total debt	-$129.06 trillion
Where the Federal Government Stands	
Net Position	-$123.11 trillion

*This includes assets reported by the government in the *Financial Report of the U.S. Government* but not all land and other assets.

With the population aging and longer life expectancy, the demographic trend is frightening. 55 million retirees over the age of 65 will become 95 million by 2060. Every year that costs trillions of dollars in Social Security and Medicare spending while younger generations are foregoing making families and having children. That equals fewer workers paying the bills.

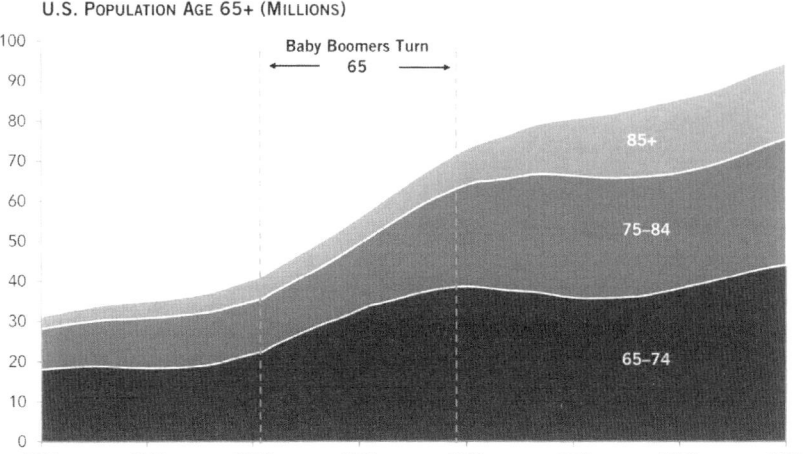

The elderly population is growing rapidly and living longer

U.S. Population Age 65+ (Millions)

SOURCES: U.S. Census Bureau, *National Intercensal Estimates*; *2016 Population Estimates*, June 2017; and *2017 National Population Projections*, September 2018.

The game is up. The Fed has already begun the process of inflating our currency and artificially manipulating the interest rates on our government debt to pay back these promises through a process of debt monetization, which otherwise would swamp the economy.

Those caught flat-footed or unprepared by the Fed monetizing the debt will suffer staggering losses in the stock market and on their savings while seeing tax rates shoot up substantially.

The Deficits Will Rise to Unsustainable Levels

With our budgets bleeding red, I know it's a prevalent groupthink or TikTok mantra to say that the Trump tax cuts led to these deficits. However, I'll remind you that **on May 7, 2014**, Federal Reserve Chairman Janet Yellen (now the Treasury Secretary under President Biden) told the Joint Economic Committee of Congress that the current federal government's deficits would rise to unsustainable levels by 2024.

CHAPTER FIVE: INFLATION ROARS BACK TO LIFE

At the time of her testimony, she stated that from 2015 to 2024 the federal government would run a $7.618 trillion deficit and the national debt would rise to $20.9 trillion.

That was 2014!

"Deficits will rise to unsustainable levels by 2024." Webster's Dictionary defines unsustainable as, "Not capable of being prolonged or continued."

Her comments came before the Covid pandemic and before the outrageous expenditures of $5.7 trillion that have been dished out. Below you'll find the chart from 2014 with the Congressional Budget Office's (CBO) projections based on government spending that she was referencing in her sworn testimony.

Before 2008, the most significant budget deficit had been around $400 billion in 2003 and 2004. By President Obama's budget, the deficit would explode on its own by 2019 to 2024.

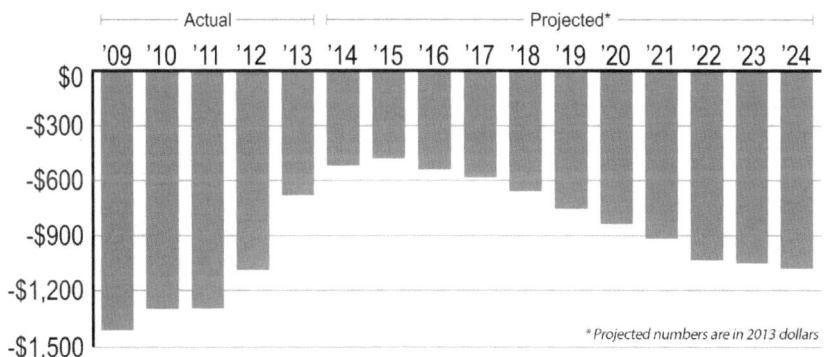

Source: Congressional Budget Office

This was one of President Obama's big talking points as he ran for reelection in 2012. "We've cut the budget deficit in half," he would tout. Naturally, that's not tough to do after monster spending bills in 2009–2011. Speaking of that time, remember that $700+ billion "stimulus bill" in March 2009 for the "Shovel Ready Jobs" which was supposed to rebuild our bridges and roads? Where did all that money go? Not to bridges and roads.

If Yellen's words were true, then how about now?

As the budget and the CBO numbers showed, the deficit projections grew in 2017 as baby boomers hit Social Security, Medicare increased, and Obamacare additional funding kicked in. These are projections that were made six years before Trump's presidency.

Keep her comments in mind for a couple of reasons.

By June 2018, the national debt eclipsed $21 trillion, six years earlier than Yellen and the Congressional Budget Office estimated. Remember, government figures, including those from the Congressional Budget Office (CBO), are always wrong. Too many variables are at play—garbage in, garbage out.

Life throws curveballs.

Secondly, there's always something unexpected that happens. The Dot-com crash. The mortgage meltdown, wars, terrorist attacks, Covid, and political leaders cramming legislation, even if it means they lose their job, because they know it will never get removed (like Obamacare).

Once a spending bill becomes part of the law, it becomes a permanent expenditure and a further expansion of the federal government. Remember, both Social Security and Medicare started as small budget expenditures, which have continued to grow.

Now Yellen says spend more!

Recall Secretary Yellen's comment from 2014 that **the deficits would be unsustainable by 2024?** Now, as Treasury Secretary, she has changed her tune, and she's in agreement that we need to spend more money.

> **RECALL SECRETARY YELLEN'S COMMENT FROM 2014 THAT THE DEFICITS WOULD BE UNSUSTAINABLE BY 2024?**

At face value, how does any of that make sense? If nothing has changed and the budget situation has worsened since the Covid pandemic began, how can it make sense to spend even more money?

Never Let a Crisis Go to Waste

I'll help you answer this one. If you've watched politicians, you will see that they adhere to what Rahm Emanuel, chief of staff during President Obama's presidency, said, "Never let a crisis go to waste."

The story of how you cook frogs comes to mind. You slowly turn up the heat, and they never notice. With great sadness, that's what is happening today. A new program is created through every crisis that costs more money and more freedom.

Since the promises of Social Security in 1935 and then Medicare and Medicaid in 1965, these programs have been unfunded. Money has been taken out of your paycheck in the form of payroll taxes to fund these programs. In 1940, there were 159 workers for every retiree, and today that number is 2.8! Plus, the enhanced benefits of Medicare and Medicaid were added in 1965 and then Obamacare in 2010.

Not only that, but we've expanded the benefits for welfare and entitlements: food stamps, unemployment, disability, earned income tax credit, child tax credit, tax credits, and other programs. They've expanded without restraint because the government can print money aided by the Fed artificially suppressing interest rates.

Examine federal budgets over time, and it's shocking. In 1965, 1% of the federal budget went towards Medicare or Medicaid, and 14% of the budget was for Social Security.

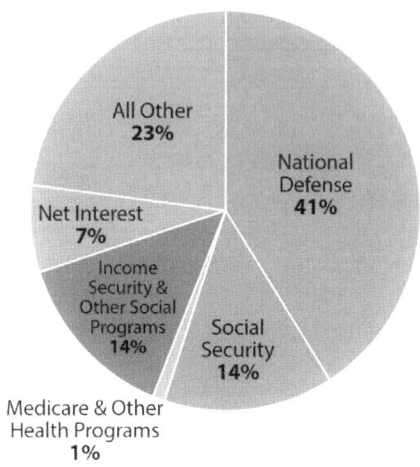

Source: Office of Management and Budget

Currently, Social Security encompasses 23% of the budget, while Medicare, Medicaid, and Obamacare-related expenditures take up 25%.

If you throw in safety-net programs like unemployment insurance, earned income credit, and others with interest on the debt, 64% of the budget is part of mandatory expenditures. Every year, these areas grow and crowd out other areas.

But notice something from the chart on the next page. 8% of the budget, outside of those areas, is for the pensions of federal employees and military veterans. Not only have mandatory programs increased, but also as the leviathan of the federal government has grown, its pension obligations have grown too.

These factors are why the Fed and the government aren't concerned about inflation.

CHAPTER FIVE: INFLATION ROARS BACK TO LIFE

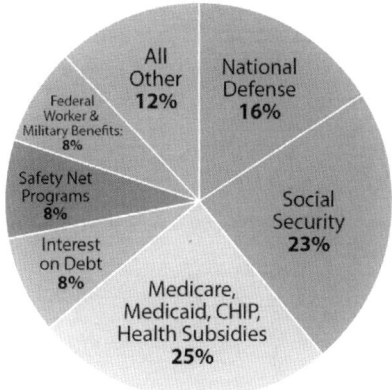

Source: Office of Management and Budget

Inflation Helps Pay Back Promises . . . With Inflated Dollars

One of the techniques I'll reveal involves locking up good debt in income-producing assets such as cash-flowing real estate, especially with the record low-interest rates we're experiencing. Then, you can repay that debt in later years with inflated dollars.

It works the same for the government too. Stay tuned for more in the next chapter.

"But David, Social Security and government pensions are indexed for inflation!"

You may find this hard to believe, but the government doesn't always do as they say. They say they're for the little guy, but their policies paint a different picture. Let me provide an example.

In 1981, the first adjustment was made to the Consumer Price Index (CPI) basket of goods, the cost-of-living index that determines adjustments to Social Security benefits—better known as Cost of Living

Adjustments (COLA). Subsequent changes occurred in 1993 and in 2010. By changing the COLA index, the federal government can stay one step ahead and use inflation to its advantage! They can use inflation to pay back promises with inflated dollars!

With inflation running 7.9% under current CPI readings, if the government were to use the 1980 basket of goods, the COLA index would be over 15%, but by using their new CPI basket of goods, Social Security recipients will receive a 5.9% increase in payments in 2022!

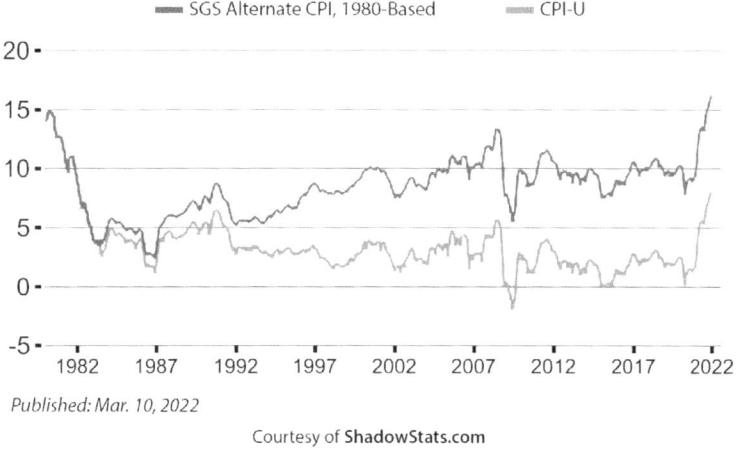

Courtesy of ShadowStats.com

For perspective, a healthy local bank receives deposits and makes money by lending that money out. A 2% spread is considered healthy and leads to riches for banks. By continually manipulating the CPI Index and creating a break from true inflation, the government limits the actual Social Security and pension payouts. Compared to the CPI of the '80s, the government today is raking in an 8% spread!

Not to be left out, federal workers and the military have been given a 2.7% COLA adjustment for 2022! This strategy is one of the ways the government uses inflation to its advantage. But it gets even worse for Social Security recipients.

Not Every Tax Bracket Is Indexed for Inflation

Chapter Four discussed the 1981 tax law change and how tax brackets were indexed for inflation in 1985. Guess whose income wasn't indexed? Retirees.

FDR had established Social Security in 1935 and said it would "never be taxed," but something happened in 1984. Congress figured out FDR had died, and they devised a system to tax Social Security.

Congress created a "provisional income calculation" of all sources of income found on the front page of a tax return, including tax-free municipal bonds, along with ½ of a retiree's Social Security.

If provisional income is over $25,000 for a single person or $34,000 for a couple, 50% of Social Security becomes subject to federal income tax. In 1993, this expanded to 85% tax for provisional incomes over $44,000. All the while, none of the income tax brackets have been indexed for inflation.

If they had been indexed, $34,000 in 1984 should be $91,000 today. It reminds me of what I previously mentioned:

The government giveth with one hand and taketh away with another!

This strategy is yet another way the government uses inflation to its advantage. This strategy worked throughout the '70s as incomes rose and tax brackets weren't indexed for inflation. Within ten years, the tax burden had doubled. But that's not the only area. It gets worse.

The 2018 Tax Cuts & Jobs Act Changed the CPI Index

Under the new tax law, the chained CPI-U Index is now used to adjust tax brackets and other deductions. Under the previous tax rules passed in 1981, the government used the CPI-U index or Consumer Price Index for Urban customers, based on a basket of goods and services. This index increases faster because inflation is recorded as prices jump for some products or services.

Chained CPI, however, incorporates substitution into the equation, thereby blunting increases. What is substitution? Let's imagine your family spends $100 a month on beef; however, beef prices increase 20%, so you alter your budget for lower-priced chicken instead of beef. Using chained CPI, this behavior change would result in no inflationary increase. Was beef 20% more expensive? Yes, but chained CPI negated the increase.

Consequently, for the tax year of 2021, tax brackets increased just over 1% from the previous year even though inflation was 7% by the CPI-U or 15% by the old 1980 CPI.

For the tax year 2022, tax brackets have increased a little over 3%. Who knows what inflation will be like in 2022, but you can guess that it will be more than 3%.

If inflation is allowed to continue its aggressive march, wage increases will outpace the chained CPI, so the tax burden will grow without politicians voting for it! It won't be as great as the "bracket creep" we saw during the '70s, but it still is an additional few percent that the government needs to keep pace with their out-of-control promises.

Other Stealth Taxes

Do you know that great tax break you receive for selling your home and not having to pay taxes on the gains? The law allows for $250,000 for individuals or $500,000 for couples to be excluded as a taxable gain. Once again, inflation is the government's friend because if this tax break were indexed to inflation, the exclusion would be $434,000 or $868,000. With soaring home values throughout the nation, the government has instituted a hidden tax through inflation.

Another stealth tax is the 2010 Obamacare 3.8% surcharge on investments and capital gains for those with incomes over $200,000 for individuals or $250,000 for couples. This amount is also unindexed to inflation.

You'll find a few unindexed items in the tax code, including the deduction for losses, which has held firm at $3,000 since its inception. Properly indexed, that deduction would be worth $13,000 today! The child tax credit is also unindexed, along with the $10,000 cap on state and local tax deductions.

Don't forget about the states!

Most states collect income tax, and only a few adjust for inflation! Over time, inflation increases the tax liability in more and more areas of life. When I say the government is a growing leviathan, believe it!

Remember the 155 people from 1969?

Don't forget, in 1969, there were 155 taxpayers who didn't pay federal taxes, yet their incomes were over $200,000 a year ($1.5 million today). Politicians were irate because these individuals had used the tax code and purchased tax-free investments to avoid the high tax rates of nearly 70% on the last dollars earned.

Because of this, Congress passed the Alternative Minimum Tax (AMT), which created a separate tax calculation beside the normal one. By 2017 nearly 5.2 million taxpayers paid a tax originally designed to catch only a few.

That's the sneaky way the government uses the tax code to achieve its goals.

The Tax Bomb Waiting in IRA's

It's one reason I've never liked the idea of Individual Retirement Accounts (IRAs) or 401(k)s. They're an excellent investment—for the government! They allow a small tax deduction on the front end and allow it to grow, sharing in the growth of the accounts via taxes on the backend.

Is a wealth tax the next to come?

Speaking of taxes, do you think Elizabeth Warren's or Bernie Sanders's ideas of wealth taxes are unimaginable?

One day soon, we'll see an expansion of the tax code with a wealth tax. And over time, just like the AMT, it will hit more and more of the population. Plus, we shouldn't fool ourselves into believing a value-added tax (or VAT) won't be too far behind. Heck, if it's good enough for Europe, it has to be good enough for us. Right?

Go ahead and get mad, or you can realize what I'm saying is true. Monumental shifts are occurring. Boys are now girls and girls are now boys. Police are viewed as criminals, and the schools are cultural indoctrination programs.

During the early Covid pandemic lockdowns, churches were deemed non-necessary and forced to close in Los Angeles, while liquor stores were allowed to be open. Could you have imagined that just a few years ago if I had told you that the government would force the closure of businesses?

> "FREEDOM IS NEVER MORE THAN ONE GENERATION AWAY FROM EXTINCTION. WE DIDN'T PASS IT TO OUR CHILDREN IN THE BLOODSTREAM. IT MUST BE FOUGHT FOR, PROTECTED, AND HANDED ON FOR THEM TO DO THE SAME."

As a dentist, health information was protected under HIPAA laws, but now, you must openly show a vaccination card in some areas of the country. No matter your feelings on Covid, vaccinated or unvaccinated, you should have the same feelings and concerns of overreach. The growth and abuse of government have only increased, and Ronald Reagan's famous quote rings true.

"Freedom is never more than one generation away from extinction. We didn't pass it to our children in the bloodstream. It must be fought for, protected, and handed on for them to do the same."

Something for nothing . . .

The bigger picture is that politicians and political leaders are denying the truth laid out before their very eyes because it benefits them.

It helps cover their wild spending sprees and promises to buy votes without having to make the tough decisions.

On the other side, Wall Street wants continued low interest rates and easy money because it's the "something for nothing" effect. The inflated monetary supply drives asset prices higher, and all the while, Wall Street is rejoicing in more trading and speculation. They don't care as long as you're trading, buying, or selling and letting them take a cut of the spread.

Larry Summers summed it up using a perfect analogy. During an interview with Bloomberg News, he said our economic policy right now is like a car going 100 mph on an uncrowded road that won't stay that way for long.

Former President Herbert Hoover said much the same. "We are now speeding down the road of wasteful spending and debt, and unless we can escape, we will be smashed in inflation."

It's not a matter of if we crash but when.

Even Ray Dalio, the famed investor, echoed Hoover's statement by noting that the options to control inflation are painful and that none of our leaders are prepared to make the tough choices. Remember the '80s? It took strong leadership by Reagan and Fed Chairman Volcker to do the unpopular.

Losing Control Happens Quickly

Losing control of any situation starts slowly, but it quickly spins out of control unless hard choices are made. Sadly, the Fed is simply fueling the fire.

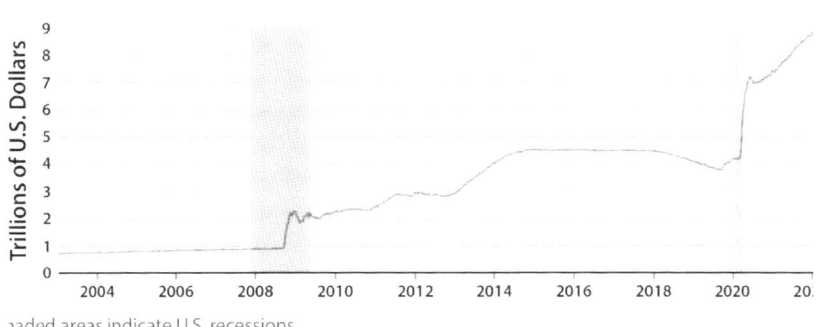

Source: Board of Governors of the Federal Reserve System (US)

Everyone agrees that the Fed's actions and involvement caused the inflation of the '70s and '80s, and today is no different. Their actions eventually lead to a bubble in the assets they're pumping or pushing that finally implodes. That's how markets work, and we've seen it throughout history.

Now, as the Fed has begun to discuss raising rates to cool the economy and inflation, the markets have gone into a nosedive!

Stock market has worst ever start to the year!

In January 2022, Chairman Powell and the FOMC announced their intentions to raise interest rates in the spring of 2022 with potentially three bumps. As the recent numbers came in and economists cried out for immediate action, the markets took notice, and January was a bloodbath for the stock market.

The Russell 2000 fell 20% from its high in November 2021, while the S&P 500 dropped 7% and the Nasdaq slumped 18%. While interest rate hikes are a concern, the market is particularly concerned about the Fed ending Quantitative Easing and its $120 billion dollars per month of purchases propping up the markets. Remember, since the Covid pandemic began, the Fed has increased its balance sheet by nearly $5 trillion.

You know things have gotten out of control when you have the taxicab driver giving you stock tips. With monster returns in 2019 of 30%, 16% in 2020, and 26% in 2021, things are out of whack.

Historically speaking, the stock market averages annual returns of 10.4%, with a lot of ups and downs that require an investor to stay invested. The last three years have been abnormal.

The entire market since 2008 has been insane when you look at what's been happening in the economy. Let's go through the charts and see what's at play.

First, let's examine the returns of the S&P 500 since 2000. We see the downturns, but the returns have been remarkable, with a few exceptions.

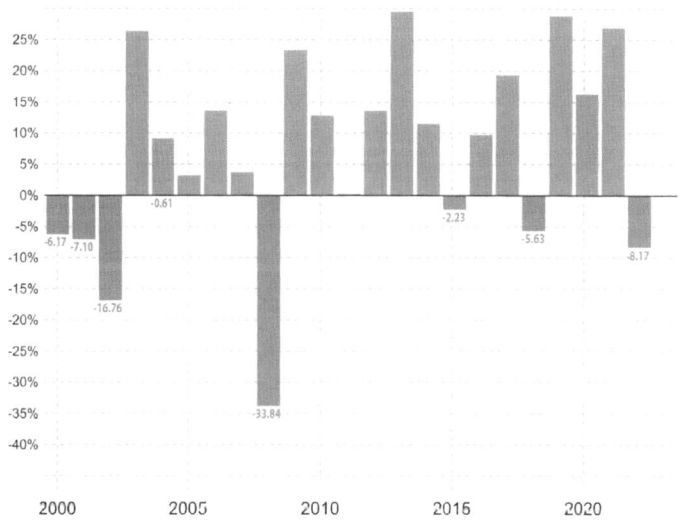

Next, the Fed's balance sheet.

FEDERAL RESERVE BALANCE SHEET

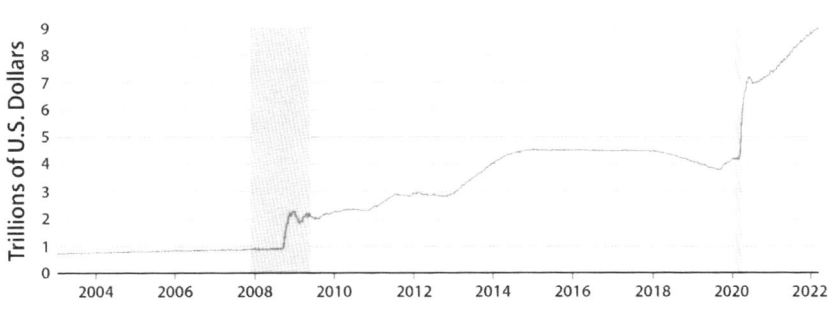

Shaded areas indicate U.S. recessions.

Source: Board of Governors of the Federal Reserve System (US)

And finally, the Fed's federal funds rate or the key dynamic for easy money.

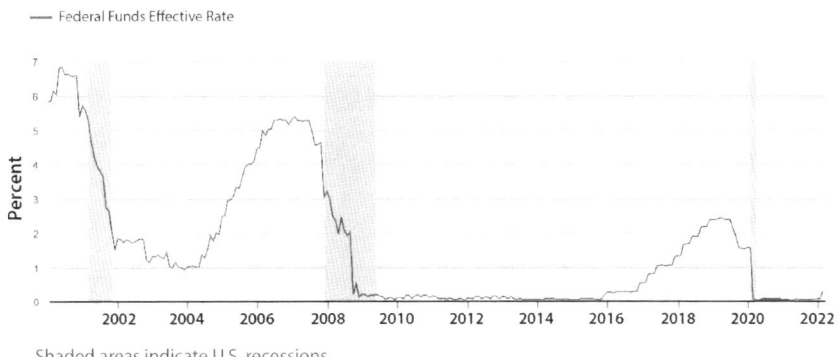

Shaded areas indicate U.S. recessions.

Source: Board of Governors of the Federal Reserve System (US)

America is on a massive sugar high that will wreak havoc on retirements and future income as inflation intensifies and the Fed is forced to withdraw money from the economy. I once again go back to the eloquent words of Milton Friedman.

"Inflation is always and everywhere a monetary phenomenon in the sense that it is and can be produced only by a more rapid increase in the quantity of money than in output."

Economically, America has entered a challenging stage of its 245-year existence. I'm concerned about the millions of hard-working families who are trying to save and prepare for the future but who have no idea of what's coming. They're still adhering to the traditional model of earn, save, and trust the stock market to grow your money. Just don't touch it or look at it.

Freedom Founders Community member Dr. Jim Rachor is a prime example. Jim grew up and learned from his dad, who was a financial advisor, so naturally, Jim followed the path his father had taught him. But something happened when he finally realized that that path wasn't working for him. Unlike many people who know that something is wrong but never take action, Jim did! Working non-stop to sock away money only to see it lost in a downturn, Jim came to a Freedom Founders event looking for a different way to build and preserve his wealth. He eventually became a Free for Life member!

At one of our events, Jim shared with the other members the changes in his portfolio since joining our community. He shared the changes he has made as he's become more comfortable with various areas of real estate and as he's transitioned out of Wall Street and into alternative investments in real estate.

As you'll learn later in Chapter Seven, Dr. Rachor and his wife have devoted a large portion of their work to the charitable foundations they operate that support children in Guatemala, a homeless shelter in Michigan, and a mentorship program for young professionals.

INFLATION: THE SILENT RETIREMENT KILLER

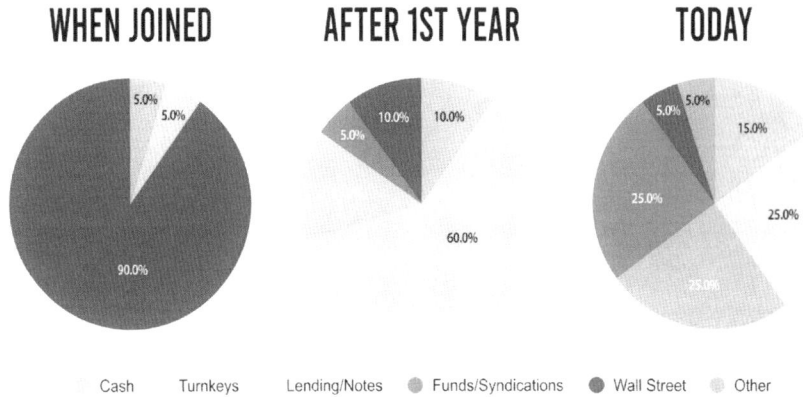

It's time to own our Freedom by planning now and by taking the necessary steps to preserve our wealth and grow it to outpace the inflation we will face in the years going forward.

I'll share the investments that outpace inflation and the strategies you can take right now to secure a firm footing. After you learn these strategies and techniques, you'll be tasked with sharing the knowledge with others. Together we can win!

Be sure to visit **www.InflationBook Resources.com**. I put together an extensive list of resources and on-time information. There are interviews with thought-leaders on inflation, investments, the future, and much more. It's free of charge and my gift to you for investing in your future!

STRATEGIES TO OFFSET THE EFFECTS OF INFLATION IN YOUR FREEDOM PLAN

CHAPTER SIX

"Inflation takes from the ignorant and gives to the well informed."
VENITA VANCASPEL, AUTHOR

"90% of all millionaires became so through owning real estate. More money has been made in real estate than in all industrial investments combined."
ANDREW CARNEGIE, STEEL TYCOON

My first rental investment property was acquired in 1980. The mortgage interest rate on the financing was 13.5%, and inflation was running hot at 14.5%. I was 23 years old, and I didn't know anything different. I didn't understand economics, interest rates, or inflation. I just wanted to get started with my first investment.

Paul Volcker had been appointed Federal Reserve Chairman to rein in the inflation that had begun in 1965 during the Johnson administration. The political will was behind him to do whatever it took. The national debt was "only" $908 billion (32% of the GDP). Volcker raised the federal funds rate to 20%, caused a stark recession, and effectively brought inflation under control.

The point is, we had a problem (inflation was out of control), and it was dealt with, notwithstanding economic hardship and pain (a national recession). This country is not in a political or fiscal position today to take a similar stance. Out-of-control debt and deficit spending have created a monster. We have effectively spent the future generations into economic slavery.

At the time of this publication, the national debt is just over $30 trillion (122% of GDP). We have no Paul Volker at the helm, and even if we did, there would be no mandate for raising interest rates to stave off inflation. We're way beyond the tipping point.

Essentially, the Federal Reserve (and our illustrious government representatives) are out of options. There's no gas left in the tank. At some point, the dollar remaining the world's reserve currency is at risk. When that is lost, all bets are off.

Volatility and chaos in the markets will rule the years to come. This will be painful and difficult to accept for the majority of hard-working Americans who have put their faith in being prudent, saving money, and investing for the most part in Wall Street financial products and retirement accounts (like 401(k)s, defined contribution, and cash balance tax-deferred plans).

For those in retirement, this volatility will be especially painful. With Wall Street's accumulation model, you must live off of what you've accumulated. That may mean you deplete your asset base as inflation requires more money to survive, and the stock market experiences jitters as we experienced throughout the '70s and early '80s. Over time, your assets may disappear entirely.

Unlike when you're younger, when the market drops 30%, it impacts your life right then and there. For many retirees, that means changing their lifestyle or going back to work. Worse yet, remember the bank certificate of deposit I showed you in the introduction that paid 12.5%? If a fixed investment came out today paying 7%, that would sound amazing in today's low interest rate environment.

What would happen if you were to lock up your money in that investment, only to see inflation and interest rates skyrocket to 13% or

14% like they did when I purchased my first property? These scenarios aren't pretty, but they're very real. **I lived through it and invested in that tumultuous time.**

The good news is that there are ways to traverse, navigate, and overcome the obstacles coming our way—but only for those willing to recognize the situation at hand and willing to go against traditional thinking and groupthink.

What to Do Now:

1. **Relationship Capital—Enhance your network with business, tax, and investment contacts and resources.**

    My best insurance policy is my digital Rolodex: the people I know. I have invested a lifetime into curating relationships across many lines of business and expertise. When I need advice, a resource, or investment opportunities, I am no more than one call or text away from the answer I need.

    Jim Rohn wisely said, "You are the average of the five people you spend the most time with." Your peers can provide you with limitless permission to make the changes you need to create more freedom in your life. In addition, your network can provide you with clarity and perspective on important decisions.

    It's no longer chic to be the John Wayne "rugged individualist." Don't be afraid to invest in yourself and join collective wisdom and influence groups. You'll gain a network of resources and your own "Board of Advisors." This is how successful people get ahead.

    In *Own Your Freedom: Sustainable Wealth for a Volatile World*, I

> **DON'T BE AFRAID TO INVEST IN YOURSELF AND JOIN COLLECTIVE WISDOM AND INFLUENCE GROUPS.**

wrote about the importance of associations and the people around us. I call it relationship capital. When we've developed quality associations, two things will occur. They'll provide us with more security, and they'll contribute to our freedom. But beware of negative associations that derail you from your goals.

I still remember, in 2010 I had sold my practice, and I was no longer inundated with the day-to-day operations of a business. Financially free and enjoying my time with my daughter Jenna, I searched for my next! How could I give back and share my experience with others? How could I share my experiences and insight with other dentists and professionals struggling to balance their work/life relationships and plan for their future?

Attending a small group mastermind meeting and sitting around a table of five, I received the inspiration and wisdom I needed. I mentioned how as a dentist I had figured out how to run a better business and get out of dentistry, I shared some of the failures I had learned along the way. I also shared my experience with real estate, which provided the passive cash flow I needed to relinquish my trading time for dollars active income as a dentist.

"I don't see how the two sides of me fit together," I told the group. "I like real estate, but I don't see how my experience in dentistry and practice management fits with my knowledge of real estate investment."

It was a young man at that table who encouraged me. Something he said hit me between the eyes. "David, you really won't know until you take some kind of step forward and test it out." He suggested holding a small gathering at my home with my circle of influence. "Share your story and see what resonates with them," he told me. Only then would I have the clarity to take the next steps.

The same is true for you.

Freedom Founders has been going strong for over ten years, changing the lives of countless dentists, professional practice owners, and other professionals. But it all began with that small mastermind at my home. As we battle the forces of inflation and other future challenges, you can't afford to go at it alone. Gather your team, join groups, and be an active participant!

For many, humility is a roadblock to success. Find associations where you can be authentic. One of the things I always hear from our Freedom Founders community is how members love our weekly Freedom Implementation Training (FIT) calls because they can lay all the cards on the table in their small group of 8 to 15 members.

The other day I hopped on a Zoom call during which a member candidly shared the discouragement he faced from the Covid pandemic. With the insane labor market we all face thanks to the inflation in wages and demand for workers, he was short five staff members, and the others were out sick when the new Covid strain appeared. After two years of battling Covid, he was at wit's end. The group responded by sharing how they overcame those same hurdles and their techniques to turn things around. As the call went on, this young dentist gleaned the wisdom of the others, and his countenance radically changed. The veil had been lifted, and he had newfound hope.

Find groups that will help you with the challenges you're facing, and make sure they stretch you! Get out of your comfort zone and get around those thinking at a higher level. What I'm telling you is: Don't be the smartest person in the room! Be humble and seek the wisdom of others to stay ahead of the changes approaching.

2. **Own or acquire an interest in business(es).**

Beyond your associations, the next key for navigating the coming inflation tsunami will be to invest in or own tangible assets such as your business or others' businesses. (Refer back to the Introduction and earlier chapters for specifics on the effects of inflation.)

Owning a well-run business allows you to increase revenues as inflation increases. As long as you have a competitive advantage or operate in an industry with solid margins, you can adjust your prices to market conditions. The last thing you want is a business focused on anything related to government incentives, tax credits, or programs.

While it may seem like a great place to be right now as the government is drunk on spending, those will be cut in the future as the mandatory expenditures of Social Security, Medicare, and Medicaid take an ever-increasing portion of the federal budget and interest on the national debt rises. If you skipped over that area, go back to Chapter Five to review the struggles we'll face as a nation as the population ages.

No doubt it takes prudence and wisdom to run a business, especially in inflationary times. Handling accounts receivables and negotiating accounts payable terms from vendors will require strategy and wisdom, but owning a business is a solid strategy for the right people. Hiring and managing staff will also pose unique challenges during these inflationary times. Still, you'll manage and succeed with the proper insight from others. Here are a few major keys to both your personal and business success you must keep in mind.

3. **Create margin (cash and cash flow) in your personal and business overhead.**

    In financial terms, having more cash on hand is what is called "strengthening the balance sheet." Cash is an asset (vs. a liability), and cash is the most fungible or liquid asset which provides both time and options. Creating more regular or recurring cash flow is known as "operating liquidity" or OpLiq for short. Operating cash flow refers to the number of months of cash available to pay the overhead expenses of a company (or personal lifestyle). Generally, three to five months is a good rule of thumb, but in times of pending recession or downturn, five to seven months may be the wiser goal.

    One of the most effective ways to address increasing inflation is to assess your expenses. Take a serious look at costs and operating expenses for both yourself (your lifestyle) and your business. You may be able to identify areas where you can make savings or cuts and create a buffer that can absorb any increased costs. (Creating more cash flow margin is very important during inflationary periods.)

Consider all aspects of your operating costs. Is it possible to source raw materials or supplies from alternative sources for a better deal? Can you set up a contract with a fixed rate to protect against increases in the near future? Is there any tolerance for adjusting your labor costs? Will you need to be able to provide a cost-of-living increase for your staff?

In your real estate investments, especially those that are leveraged acquisitions with debt financing, being prepared is the best defense against the potential for rising costs and inflation. It is far better to assess your budget and operating costs now rather than when you are under pressure to make cuts when prices start to increase.

4. **Be nimble, adaptable, and able to pivot as needed (business and personal).**

The ability to make rapid changes as needed is a point of strength during periods of market and economic uncertainty. Consider reducing extravagant plans for increases in fixed costs, including expanding your office or your own home. Keep an eye on staffing, or other long-term commitments that can't be easily terminated.

Maintaining an efficient labor force (staffing) is also ideal in preparing for a shifting market. Labor is one of the highest costs for any business. In a stagnant economy with high inflation (stagflation), any expenses that can be reduced will allow for room to shift tactics and strategies to maintain market viability.

Now is a time in the business cycle when "getting more from fewer and less" should be a standing mantra. Be willing to invest more in fewer but higher output people, contractors, or vendors. Fewer and better means less to manage and the ability to work with those self-motivated people who already come with high standards and don't need to be managed.

The one unique difference between the '70s and '80s and today is the shortage of workers. While labor unions were a primary driver of wage increases in the past, today it's the limited supply of qualified workers. With eleven million unfilled jobs, everyone is fighting over quality workers.

To win, you must recruit and look for staff, so you're not caught flat-footed. Network and keep an eye out for top-notch workers. Create a culture and environment that rewards the employee and drives retention. Others can and will always offer higher wages; however, the right combination of work environment, atmosphere, and flexibility can easily overcome pay obstacles.

5. **Remove dependence on variable rate financing.**

   Business or personal lines of credit are useful tools during times of economic growth. However, in an economic downturn or recession, credit markets tighten (liquidity is reduced), which often means that open lines of credit are canceled or greatly reduced by the lender (creditor).

   During the 2008 downturn, one acquaintance of mine learned this the hard way. Ken owned a commercial contracting company in St. Louis, and they had a $2 million line of credit from their local bank. From this account, they would purchase supplies and then repay the loan once the jobs were completed.

   One day he learned the hard way that when times get tough, banks recall their credit lines. In doing so, the bank used "offset" to repay the loan, draining his business account, which was also at the same bank. I know we love to think that our relationships with banks are important, but you're only a number in most cases. One strategy to keep in mind is to keep your debt and asset accounts at different banks, if possible.

The best moves to counteract lack of credit are to 1) pay off any existing variable rate loans or lines of credit and/or 2) see if the creditor will allow you to turn an open line of credit balance into a fixed-rate amortizing loan. 3) Refer back to Strategy #1—Relationship Capital. The ability to de-finance or refinance debt on a property with private capital is an option that most investors have never considered. A network of financial friends provides a level of safety and antifragility that can never be gained from institutional relationships.

In other words, don't be caught with credit that can easily be terminated. Cash flow is king during economic corrections, and you don't want to have to use cash to pay off open credit lines if at all possible.

Finally, remember the rules of banking. A bank will always lend money when you don't need it, but you can never get it when you need it! Think and act with this rule in mind.

6. **Short the Dollar—Lock in long-term, low-rate fixed financing on capital investments.**

    The use of long-term fixed-rate financing to acquire strong cash-flowing assets (businesses or real estate) is an arbitrage position. By using historic low-interest rates to own cash-flowing assets, you can arbitrage or "take the spread" between the low financing rates and the cash flow of the investment asset.

    Consider the math: The inflation rate as measured by the Consumer Price Index reached 7% in December 2021. With the *nominal federal funds rate* effectively at zero (0.25%), that translates into a *real funds rate* of -7%. That's a *minus* seven (-7%), in case you didn't catch it.

    That is a record low.

    Only twice before in modern history, early 1975 and again in mid-1980, was the real funds rate close to today's -7%. During both of those years, '75 and '80, the real rate was -5% (the federal funds rate minus the rate of inflation). Those two instances encapsulated a five-year-plus period of inflation over which the CPI rose at an 8.6% average annual rate.

And here we are today at -7%.

A -7% real interest rate is almost sci-fi. It doesn't make sense. *It means anyone who can borrow at the federal funds rate or close to it is effectively being paid to take on more debt.* And not just paid but paid well, plus whatever return they can generate with the borrowed money. This is partly why so many asset prices are so bubble-like today.

As an example, if one can borrow long-term (for a minimum of ten years, ideally 25 or 30 years) at fixed interest rates of, say, 4% on cash-flowing assets that produce quantifiable cash flow returns, it actually pays to borrow. The nominal rate of 4% minus the inflation rate (CPI) of 7% equals a real rate of -3%. And assuming the cap rate (the return on that asset) cash flows at 6% (which is low for the real estate in which we invest in Freedom Founders), then my real rate of return is 9% (6% + 3%). I just got an additional 3% cash flow return by playing the game.

That's not just an additional 3%! That's a 50% increase in return over the actual 6%. Does this make sense? I know, hard to believe, but this is the bizarro world in which we find ourselves today. If you don't understand this concept, you are going to be very disappointed in your investments over the next several decades. One day, you will ask yourself, "How could this have happened?"

The sleight of hand of the sneaky Federal Reserve. It's how the wealth transfer occurs without anyone holding a gun to your head. No one directly confiscated your money or assets. They took it in the middle of the night when you didn't even see it coming.

Let me say that again, in case you missed the point. With the right asset, with the right financing, it pays to borrow! No, Dave Ramsey will never teach this principle, but he's not advocating for business entrepreneurs and sophisticated investors; he helps mainstream

America balance their checkbooks. If you're reading this book, you don't need the well-intentioned basics that Ramsey professes.

This is where real estate as a long-term investment asset shines. Utilizing financing leverage to acquire the property allows for rapid net worth growth and subsequent cash flows. (It's all about the cash flow—don't let anyone tell you otherwise in regards to your investments.)

As inflation increases, so will interest rates. However, fixed-rate interest rate financing does not change over time; it is "fixed" for the duration of the loan. As a result, as inflation causes the value or purchasing power of the dollar to be reduced (as explained in the Introduction), you are actually "shorting the dollar." The dollars that you use in the future to pay your financing debt will be accomplished with dollars of reduced value.

7. Use a Currency Converter to offset the devaluation of the dollar

People who are on "fixed income" (like from social security, interest returns on savings accounts, etc.) are those who will suffer most in an inflationary environment. As noted previously, in an inflationary environment of 12%, the purchasing power of the dollar will decrease by 50% in only six years.

What would happen to your lifestyle if every six years, you had half the income to provide the means for your living costs? It might not take too many cycles of this income reduction before you would be rendered to government assistance.

What if you had a "currency converter?" A mechanism that would take your current nest egg investment capital and convert it into the same purchasing power in six years, twelve years, or even twenty years without having to add to the nest egg?

That's exactly what tangible assets like real estate will do. You purchase or invest in real estate with today's dollars at today's values and as inflation increases, so does the value of your nest egg—more importantly, so does the cash flow produced from that nest egg (in the form of real estate equity).

For example, if I own an investment property today valued at $150,000.00 that produced a net cash flow return (after subtracting all expenses) of $800 per month (dollar currency 1.0), and in five years, with inflation running at 12%, that same investment property is now worth $264,000.00 AND the net cash flow has also increased to $1,360 per month, I haven't lost the purchasing power of my dollars to inflation. They have been converted to "new dollar currency 2.0."

8. **Re-allocate and diversify qualified retirement accounts into tangible assets.**

   Most retirement accounts are invested in the stock market. That is the default method of retirement planning. The downside is that financial assets are at the greatest risk of volatility and loss during economic recessions and high inflation.

   Go back to the Introduction or Chapter Five to see how what you may hear from Wall Street and the financial pornography on TV is biased. It's flat-out wrong and deceitful. From 1969 to 1982, the stock market returns were 5.3% per year but -1.8% after adjusting for inflation. This period of investing was known as "the Lost Decade." It included some horrific drops reminiscent of the Dot-com crash and the mortgage meltdown.

CHAPTER SIX: STRATEGIES TO OFFSET THE EFFECTS OF INFLATION IN YOUR FREEDOM PLAN

Source: Macrotrends.net

A viable strategy for qualified retirement accounts is to move the assets (money) to a licensed custodian that allows you, the owner (fiduciary of the account), to self-direct into alternative, tangible investments. In the Freedom Founders Community, this change is one of the first tactical moves that our members complete.

There are a myriad of licensed and IRS-approved custodians in the U.S. that provide for the self-direction of qualified retirement accounts such as traditional IRAs, Roth IRAs, Health Savings Accounts, and 401(k)s. Don't allow those retirement accounts to remain in an uncontrolled and historically volatile Wall Street environment. It is your responsibility to advocate for your future.

Diversifying into tangible assets in a retirement account provides for greater stability and a wider degree of asset diversification.

9. **Collaboration**—Learn how to create collaborations with others who have niche opportunities for capital investment.

Investing in Relationship Capital also provides for collaborative relationships. Finding people who bring different ideas, skill sets, or experience can provide the synergy to produce better and faster results.

In our Freedom Founders mastermind community, one of our veteran doctors made the point that he was able to easily borrow money (capital) from another member's self-directed IRA account. He didn't need to go to a bank (who would have put him through all kinds of hoops, underwriting, appraisals, fees, etc.) when his personal relationship with another person allowed him to expedite his wealth-building plan. At the same time his friend was able to earn interest in his qualified retirement account.

This sort of collaboration is how we can essentially eliminate having to rely on the traditional financial markets.

In my own personal experience of building a real estate portfolio over many years, I only used private capital as my financial leverage point. It was safe; it was much easier, and I created lifetime relationships that allowed me to have access to capital even when the retail markets were not lending.

In my experience, far too many people don't understand the art of collaboration and instead believe that owning or controlling an opportunity provides the greatest personal outcome. I have found the opposite to be true. Bringing complementary benefits to a business or investment opportunity with the right person or people can significantly enhance the overall results. The sum of many is greater than the individual parts.

Look for people who are "long game" in perspective. In other words, beware of those who are focused only on "what's in it for them" and how they get paid on the front end. The best collaborators are those who are able to be patient and see a project through to completion without the necessity of short-term incentives.

My Favorite Is Real Estate

What I know is that the optimal route for success during inflationary times is the time-tested asset class of real estate. Having been invested in real estate since the last inflationary period of the early '80s, I understand why real estate has won out through good times and bad. Remember, I purchased my first rental property when interest rates were 13.50% and inflation was burning hot at 14.50%. My first property still cash flowed, and I made a lot of money.

But it's not only cash flow where real estate wins. Real estate provides tax benefits, amortization benefits, growth, and income which many investors don't know about. Real estate is the ultimate financial foundation, and it gets even better if you've financed properties and locked up your loans with fixed mortgages.

Benefits of Real Estate

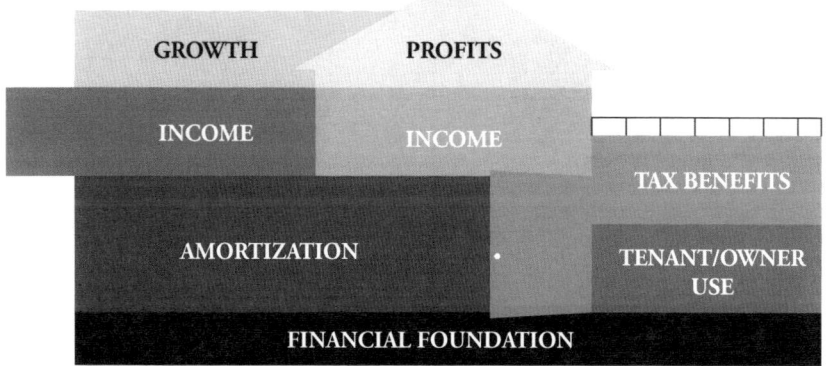

Diagram courtesy of Pete Fortunato

Time magazine ran an article in January of 1981 called: "Inflation: The Enemy is Us." It went on to say that "homeowners are among the biggest gainers" from high inflation. I love these first-hand accounts from this time period.

The article went on to talk about how inflation offers handsome benefits to some. Who's the some? Real estate owners. It also zeroes in on what I suggested earlier, locking in loans at today's low rate and repaying it with inflated dollars.

"Borrowers can now repay their debts with dollars' worth just .63¢ in 1975 terms."

The other benefit is that real estate values rise with inflation, along with cash flow. Think about it. Besides food, people must have a roof over their heads, whether in single-family homes or apartment buildings. As commodities and materials such as lumber, copper, concrete, and steel rise in price, the prices of homes rise in a similar fashion. And don't get caught up on interest rates because the name of the game is buying the right property in the right location with great cash flow.

Here's a view of the Case-Shiller Home Price Index compared to inflation and wealth expansion. You'll find that over time, real estate prices have doggedly tracked inflation and wealth expansion since post-WWII.

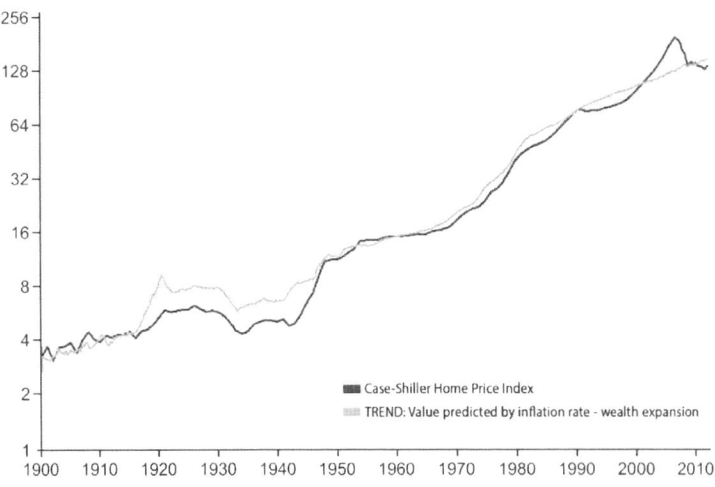

Better yet, as home prices increase, many would-be buyers are priced out of the market and are forced to rent. Just look at today and the recent headline on **February 20th, 2022**, in the *Daily Mail* newspaper. The article headline reads, "Rent across America's biggest cities soar by 20% last year due to pent-up demand from young people combined with a national housing shortage."

Of course, in today's low interest rate environment, it makes a ton of sense to lock up your loan in a long-term low-interest rate loan and pray for inflation! You'll be repaying the loan with inflated dollars, as Time magazine wrote about in 1981. But there's an even better way to propel your financial future in real estate.

A Word about Leverage

One of the many reasons I love real estate is because it allows you to use financial leverage to grow your net worth and cash flow. Because of the stability of real estate throughout history, even during volatile market cycles, financing has always been available. The use of financing to acquire and control capital assets allows for a force multiplier. The investor's cash flow return on their actual cash investment is enhanced, as are the tax benefits (another benefit of tangible assets), plus the growth or equity component.

Instead of working fifteen years longer to generate another $1.2 million in savings or 401(k) contributions, the use of financial leverage will increase the speed at which the Freedom Number is reached. Remember, the metric that matters most is passive cash flow, not accumulation. By focusing on the cash flow, the dollar amount of assets to create that cash flow is far less than the traditional guidance provided by financial advisors. This simple shift and rejection of traditional thinking literally changes the lives of those who learn to implement it. All fear and uncertainty are removed.

To understand leverage, let's compare two strategies. Suppose a single-family home rental is purchased for $100,000 and rented out for $1,200 per month or $14,400 per year. Of course, it's not all profit. An investor must account for operating expenses, including repairs, maintenance, insurance, and property taxes. The amount remaining after expenses is referred to as the Net Operating Income or "NOI." In this example, the annual NOI is $8,640 for this single rental ($14,400 x 60%).

By utilizing leverage, the same $100,000 can purchase five homes each worth $100,000 with 20% down ($20,000 x 5) while securing a 30-year mortgage for the remaining 80%. After subtracting operating expenses and debt service, the NOI results in $3,312 per year per home or a total of $16,560 for the five houses. This is almost a 100% increase in cash flow utilizing the same $100,000, and we haven't even considered price appreciation, amortization, or depreciation offset.

Leverage Vs. No Leverage

$100K No Leverage - Single $100K Home		
$100K	+	$100K Cash Purchase
	−	$1,200 / Mo Rental Income
		40% Operational Expenses
	=	**$8,640 / Yr.** N.O.I.

$100K Leveraged - Five $100K Homes		
$20K	−	$20K Down per Home
	−	$80K Finance per Home @5.3%
$20K	+	$1,200 / Mo Rental Income per Home
	−	40% Operational Expenses
$20K	−	$444 Debt Service per Home
$20K	=	$3,312 / Yr. N.O.I. per Home
$20K		
	x	5 Homes
	=	**$16,560 / Yr.** N.O.I.

CHAPTER SIX: STRATEGIES TO OFFSET THE EFFECTS OF INFLATION IN YOUR FREEDOM PLAN

The best example I can provide is from my friend who shared his dad's old bank certificate paying 12.5% in 1982. He pulled out his parent's home papers, and we crunched some numbers one day. Their home, 3037 Smiley, was purchased in 1957 for $15,800. In 1991, his parents sold the home for $139,900. In a 34-year period of time, the property's value had appreciated **785%!**

3037 Smiley Road
$139,900

Rooms: 9
Living Room: 20x15
Kitchen: 11x11
Bedroom 2: 15x11
Total square footage: 2,052

Bedrooms: 4
Dining Room: 26x11
Breakfast Room: 8x8
Bedroom 3: 12x11

Baths: 2
Family Room: 21x9
Bedroom 1: 15x11
Bedroom 4: 11x11
Property taxes: $1,086 (1992)

Utilities:

Heat: 150,000 BTU forced-air gas furnace
A/C: 48,000 BTU electric central air conditioner
Avg. electric bill: $63.92/mo.
Avg. trash bill: N/A (provided free by the City of Bridgeton)

Water Heater: Electric
Avg. gas bill: $31.50/mo.
Avg. water bill: $7.50/mo.

Schools

Bridgeway Elementary
Pattonville Jr. High
St. Blase Parish
Pattonville Sr. High

For more information, call Greg Jordan (994-8221) or Derek Gilbert (994-8555).

Over that same period, inflation increased 385%. That property's value outpaced inflation by more than two-to-one. **That is the power of real estate done right.**

Investing in tangible, revenue-producing real estate has been my model to build and grow wealth for over four decades, and it has never let me down. At Freedom Founders, we're constantly adjusting and, what I call, "moving the platter" to balance investments among different asset classes of real estate. Tangible assets like real estate are not only the best hedge against inflation but also an essential hedge against volatility in the rest of the market.

> **INVESTING IN TANGIBLE, REVENUE-PRODUCING REAL ESTATE HAS BEEN MY MODEL TO BUILD AND GROW WEALTH FOR OVER FOUR DECADES, AND IT HAS NEVER LET ME DOWN.**

Suppose you put your money blindly into the market, 401(k), or a cash balance defined-benefit plan. In that case, you're abdicating control of your future to the whims of the highly manipulated and unpredictable stock market.

With real estate, the model has worked for me over four decades through up-markets, down-markets, and sideways-markets. It works because I control my capital and deploy it at the right time in the inefficient market of real estate where buyers and sellers don't have the same information. In real estate, it's who you know and what you know!

Real Estate Is More Than Rental Properties

My final note on real estate is that you'll find it's much more than rental properties. There are various asset classes of real estate, from lending and notes to funds and syndications to turnkey rentals and other strategies. Your strategy over time should change as market conditions change.

During the mortgage meltdown, I switched and pursued a strategy of purchasing distressed debt for pennies on the dollar. Today, I'm more invested in syndications. As the captain of your ship, playing a role in your financial future, you'll use on-time information to determine the routes and strategies that make sense for you and your Freedom Blueprint™.

During our member events at Freedom Founders, a few members share their investment strategies and portfolios over time. It's incredible to see the different routes people take with their investments. The pie chart below is how one of our members expanded their portfolio as their comfort level grew with different real estate asset classes.

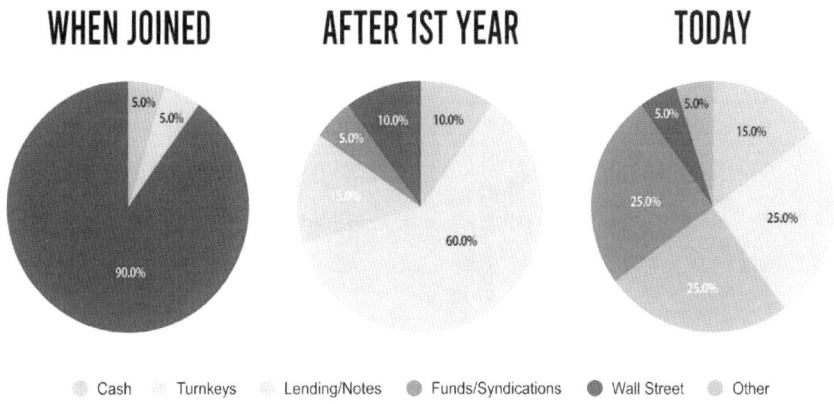

Do Your Due Diligence!

At the end of the day, the most important factor when investing in real estate is the track record of the deal sponsor and the due diligence you'll perform. **We're not financial advisors or managers at Freedom Founders, and we don't sell investments.** Instead, we're high-level educators and connectors.

Over my four decades of real estate investing, I've built a network of deal sponsors I've invested and worked with. I also believe in vetting anyone before investing with them and before bringing them into the Freedom Founders Community as a Trusted Advisor.

The novice investor believes it would be an affront or disrespectful to ask the "hard questions" that absolutely should be asked before turning over one's hard-earned money to someone else. That is precisely why we read time and time again about a real estate manager or promoter swindling people out of their hard-earned dollars.

Over the years, simply by being involved in multiple real estate, business, and investor mastermind groups, I have curated a vast network of potential investment opportunities. The keyword is "potential." Before I jump in with anyone, I have my securities attorney run a full background check on the principals in the business. How many other people do that? My guess is next to none.

But that's not all. If the background check is clear, the next step is to evaluate the track record or performance of the principal (deal sponsor) in the specific asset class they promote. The due diligence checklist we use in Freedom Founders is four pages long! This is an essential step in evaluating where you invest.

Here's where the rubber meets the road. Anyone can look like a genius in a bull market like we've had in the last few years. I have deal sponsors approach me every week touting their "returns." What I want to see is how they've done during market downturns.

Many sponsors haven't been in business that long. A vast majority have yet to experience a credit crunch or market hiccup. That's why it's important to ask the tough questions and have a team to help you evaluate deals and opportunities. Haven't you noticed that everyone seems to have a "can't miss" opportunity?

Take Action & Take Control of Your Future

Parked cars never move. Information without action is delusion. I've laid out the facts about the inflationary cycle we're entering. I've shown you the strategies to achieve success. Now it's time to act.

Let's pretend I'm wrong and say inflation soon subsides. If you've used my strategies of owning your own profitable business or investing in alternative investments in real estate, you're no worse off.

But if I'm right (and I'm pretty sure that if you've made it this far my presentation of data and analysis of the situation have struck a chord with you), then it's time to take action. I mentioned earlier the Twin Towers and the terrorist attack of 9/11. How many stories did we hear of people who were told to go back to their office and that everything was fine? The smart ones acted on intuition and took action to escape the coming calamity of the buildings collapsing. Right now, the warning sirens are blasting. It's your choice from here.

CHAPTER SIX: STRATEGIES TO OFFSET THE EFFECTS OF INFLATION IN YOUR FREEDOM PLAN

In the final chapter, I want to introduce you to other professionals, just like you, who have found freedom by using the strategies and concepts I've shared with Freedom Founders members for over ten years. With a plan and direction, they've been able to reach financial freedom in two to four years by taking what I've learned over forty years of investing and following my path.

Now it's your turn!

Remember to visit **www.InflationBook Resources.com** to access additional information and resources. I put these together to help you on this journey to win the fight against inflation. There are interviews with thought-leaders on inflation, investments, the future, and much more. It's free of charge and my gift to you for investing in your future!

CHAPTER SEVEN

LIVES TRANSFORMED BY SUSTAINABLE PASSIVE INCOME—THE FREEDOM FOUNDERS MODEL

Wake-up calls, when they come, at first seem painful. I still remember that day in the hospital waiting room when my daughter Jenna was undergoing her liver transplant. For others, the wake-up call may come in the form of uncertainty or retirement, burnout in their careers, concerns about the stock market, or the loss of that special time with their family as children grow up.

At Freedom Founders, I'm privileged to work with many dentists, professional practice owners, and professionals who have shunned conventional thinking and embraced their own paths to freedom utilizing strategies found outside of Wall Street. In the process, they've overcome obstacles in their own lives and created the future they desired.

> **IN THE PROCESS, THEY'VE OVERCOME OBSTACLES IN THEIR OWN LIVES AND CREATED THE FUTURE THEY DESIRED.**

Many of their obstacles are the same ones you're probably facing right now, so I want to introduce you to just a few of them. Many others can be found on my website **www.FreedomFounders.com** or on my YouTube Channel, but I just want to share a few of their amazing stories.

Dr. Greg and Jackie Linney's Journey to Retirement Clarity & Certainty

In 2019, Dr. Greg Linney and his amazing wife Jackie were on the cusp of selling their practice, nestled in an affluent suburb of Houston, Texas. Everything seemed in place for retirement except one thing.

Would they have enough money to make it through?

No matter how they ran the numbers, Greg wasn't confident that he could replace his working income with sustainable cash flow from his investments even in the best-case scenarios. He summarized his situation by saying,

"I was forced to accept that either I would have to reduce our family lifestyle or draw down our retirement savings and 'hope' that our nest egg outlasted us. Our "wake-up call" was that we could not afford to have both our home and our vacation home in Palm Springs—a place filled with many memories and a place we love. Retirement, as it was, would force us to sell one of them."

It was this turning point that led them to investigate Freedom Founders.

Jackie tells the story best. When they first checked out Freedom Founders, she was adamant there was, "no way we'd be joining." By the end of the first day, surrounded by so many other like-minded professionals who had faced and overcome the same dilemmas, Jackie told Greg they needed to jump in and begin their journey to freedom.

The rest is history and Greg openly shares how things have changed.

"Today, our retirement is secured by real, tangible assets. Not only that, but we have completely replaced our significant practice income with sustainable, predictable cash flow from our investments."

Even when the Covid pandemic hit and other friends were reeling from the stock market roller coaster, their passive income kept coming in steadily every month. Best of all, they were able to keep their beautiful Palm Springs home and enjoy it in retirement.

Dr. Jim Rachor's Flight to Freedom and Time for Charity

Another great example of embracing the wake-up call and deciding to go against tradition and conventional wisdom is my friend Dr. Jim Rachor. Jim's dad was a financial advisor, and that belief in the stock market carried through until Jim realized, exactly what I had realized years before, that the market seemed like a rigged game.

"I felt like I was going to a casino and betting on red or black," Jim said. "One day the market was up and I made money and the other days I lost money."

Working 12-hour days, including a lot of Saturdays, he was making money and saving, but he couldn't realize the freedom that should have come with the money. All he knew was to earn and save and someday he'd hopefully hit some magical number that would be enough. But how much was that? When would that occur? One day he read my book, *From High Income to High Net Worth*, and it all clicked. The mindset shift was immediate.

"David talked about 'living a legacy' not leaving a legacy and it hit me hard. If I could live a legacy with the kids right now, instead of later in life, I could make an impact now and in the future."

Jim realized he had been shackled by a scarcity mindset and had never considered investments that could provide cash flow on a monthly basis to create passive income. "I wasn't happy and I wasn't free in my practice. All I did was work work work while hoping for that day I might be free."

Once he sat down and designed his Freedom Blueprint™, he had the certainty in the numbers he desired with his Freedom Number. With passive income replacing his active income and the mindset shift that occurred within Freedom Founders, he fine-tuned his practice to create the life he desired.

Today, Dr. Rachor is Free for Life,™ and he actively participates and mentors others. "It's really transformed my life. I'm no longer chained to my practice and can rest easy knowing that I don't have to depend on Wall Street to reach my financial goals."

But his impact goes far beyond Freedom Founders or his own life. He and his wife started a foundation in Guatemala called Transforming Futures along with a mentorship program for young practitioners called the Smile Mentorship Institute. They also perform dental procedures in Flint Michigan at a homeless shelter.

> "I FINALLY REALIZED THAT IF YOU WANT AN EXTRAORDINARY RETIREMENT AND TRUE FREEDOM RIGHT NOW, YOU CANNOT USE 'ORDINARY' INVESTMENTS."

"I finally realized that if you want an extraordinary retirement and true freedom right now, you cannot use 'ordinary' investments."

Dr. Hiru and Sumit Mathur's Journey to Financial Freedom

As a busy Periodontist, wife, and mom, Dr. Mathur's wake-up call was the good that came from the Covid pandemic. While confined at home due to the pandemic, Hiru got a glimpse of what life could be like if she wasn't working full time at her practice.

Hiru and her husband Sumit, who runs a software business, are the typical high-performing professionals who are blessed with drive and determination, but they were shackled by traditional thinking that says: Sacrifice time with your family to earn a living and save for retirement then turn that money over to Wall Street, and eventually, you can take your foot off the pedal.

But something was missing. That something was time with her family.

They had come to the conclusion that Wall Street was letting them down and had started down the road of real estate, even buying programs of some of the well-known real estate gurus out there. Unfortunately,

CHAPTER SEVEN: LIVES TRANSFORMED BY SUSTAINABLE PASSIVE INCOME—THE FREEDOM FOUNDERS MODEL

they soon discovered that they were expected to canvas neighborhoods on the weekend searching for "deals" and coordinate "fix and flips."

Not exactly a good fit for two professionals who were already working full time.

That's when a fellow dentist opened Hiru's eyes to what was possible and introduced her to Freedom Founders. As they began to invest in passive cash flow-producing real estate, options began to unfold. At their Freedom Blueprint™ strategy session, Hiru realized that she was in a position to bring in another associate, rather than selling her practice, buy back some of her time, and reallocate it to her family.

She had expected a reduction in income that would be replaced by the passive cash flow from her alternative investments in real estate. Instead, she found her income went up as she added new hires, and she's learned how to build wealth outside of her practice.

"I can now take my foot off the pedal and start to own my freedom. I'm going to own my freedom now. Not in 10 years. Not in 15 years. I'm going to own it now. And that means I get the opportunity to make some decisions differently today than I would have a year ago."

> "I CAN NOW TAKE MY FOOT OFF THE PEDAL AND START TO OWN MY FREEDOM. I'M GOING TO OWN MY FREEDOM NOW.

The wake-up call of the Covid pandemic turned into a blessing, and she's once again enjoying her practice and work because she discovered wealth outside of Wall Street in alternative investments in real estate. Moreover, through her mindset shift and the support of the entire collaborative team at Freedom Founders, she's become an exceptional leader!

Dr. Ben & Sondra Jensen from Darkness to Light

Dr. Ben Jensen had reached the lowest of lows. He had fired his entire staff, and he wasn't happy. In fact, he just wanted to quit. Owning a small rural practice, Ben realized that selling his practice and riding into the sunset wasn't an option, and he looked at the second half of his career with dismay and fear.

"I was in a dark place. I wasn't happy and I wanted a way out, but I couldn't see any light."

Ben and Sondra had struggled to find an investing strategy that would allow them to achieve their goals. They had hired a couple of consultants and joined a few masterminds, but nothing really gave them the peace of mind they desired. Worse yet, nothing created the cash flow they knew they needed to replace Ben's practice income.

> "I WAS IN A DARK PLACE. I WASN'T HAPPY AND I WANTED A WAY OUT, BUT I COULDN'T SEE ANY LIGHT."

When they first were introduced to Freedom Founders and came to an event, Sondra was adamant, just like many spouses: "We're not making a decision this weekend," she said. At the end of the first day that had all changed, and their journey to freedom began.

Today, Ben and Sondra are Free for Life™ and a testament to what can occur in anyone's life if they're open to new information and thought. In fact, with the mindset shift that occurred, Ben cut his practice days down, and his income increased! A typical story within the community.

Additionally, Ben felt the confidence of his Freedom Implementation Team (FIT) and their weekly accountability and advice. "It's a powerful thing to have smart people that I know, like and trust weighing in on my investments and my strategies."

CHAPTER SEVEN: LIVES TRANSFORMED BY SUSTAINABLE PASSIVE INCOME—THE FREEDOM FOUNDERS MODEL

Could You Be Next? It's Possible!

These stories should inspire you and help you realize, "It's Possible!"

But every day, time marches by. Is it time to make changes in your life and investments? Are you ready to reclaim your time and availability for your family?

Whatever you do, don't fall into the trap of groupthink and conventional skepticism by saying it won't work for you. Instead, take the steps necessary to enjoy Freedom!

> **ARE YOU READY TO RECLAIM YOUR TIME AND AVAILABILITY FOR YOUR FAMILY?**

I urge you to begin to realize what Dr. Tom Jovicich shared during one of our Freedom Founders events:

"I would say you need to be able to think outside the box. Because the path you're on currently is in a box. Your family, your church, your life, your business—these are all within a certain box. And if you're so ingrained in working within that box, you get very comfortable, which also means you get blindsided by disruption."

If you're ready to step outside the box and go in a new direction, schedule a call to speak with my team. You'll attain more *clarity of where you are and a clearer vision of where you need to be* in 45 minutes than you have had your entire life. Call my office (972) 203-6960 or go online to schedule. **www.FreedomFounders.com/Schedule**

From there, if you're a fit and someone who is interested in joining the anti-traditional Freedom Founders Community, you can explore it from there by joining us at a member event. Your only risk is not checking it out for yourself!

ABOUT THE AUTHOR

DR. DAVID PHELPS

Who Is Dr. David Phelps? And Why Should You Listen To Him?

A Practice Owner Turned CEO and Leader

David owned and managed a private practice dental office for over 21 years before his daughter's health crisis served as a dramatic wake-up call in his life. David's "Plan B" (a portfolio of cash-flow producing real estate assets) gave him the Freedom to sell his practice mid-career and focus 100% on what matters most to him.

David does not follow the majority but lives life and does business on his own terms and is not dictated to by others.

America's #1 Authority on Creating Freedom in Life and Business

David is the author of seven published business, finance, and success books. As a nationally recognized keynote speaker, David brings dynamic energy and unique insights into how to create financial freedom through passive income, how to build a real business that doesn't take over your life, anti-traditional real estate investing, private lending, wealth-building legacy, and how to take responsibility and "own" your life.

A Leader Born through Crisis

Sitting with his daughter in the hospital room after her battle with leukemia and a life-saving liver transplant, Dr. David Phelps realized what matters most. It was not his career as a dentist that had consumed his daily life for over 21 years. He needed to be present for his daughter, Jenna.

He decided he would no longer practice dentistry. Instead, he was able to pivot to his Plan B.

He drew inspiration from his years of investing avidly in real estate that began during his time in dental school with a joint-venture investment with his father. By leveraging the lessons and capital he had acquired, David built an investment portfolio that could generate enough passive income to leave his dental practice and be the father his daughter needed.

An Escapee of the Dollars-For-Hours Trap

David's radical new life intrigued his peers, who asked him how they too could command control of their wealth and time. By bringing together his two worlds—high-income medical professionals and real estate professionals—David created a powerful network of like-minded professionals who could support each other on their own paths to financial and personal freedom.

He called this group Freedom Founders, and as its leader, he found his purpose: helping his colleagues break the chains of bondage to their practices and financial fears and create freedom in their lives.

With his own life as proof, David challenges the traditional model of wealth building, which preaches abdicating control over one's money to advisors and entrusting all of one's investing capital to Wall Street.

David has witnessed too many high-income professionals blindly trust the traditional path only to have their hard-earned wealth wiped out by the volatility of the public market. Through Freedom Founders, David exhorts his members to take back control of their investing capital from their practices and 401(k) plans, put it to work in more stable, capital-producing assets like real estate, and always stay focused on their own freedom.

Free for Life™

Freedom Founders Mastermind Group began as a meeting of sixteen people over a decade ago and has grown into a community of over 100 members and Trusted Advisors, where David's insights into the financial markets, alternative investing, and achieving success and fulfillment in life attract freedom-seeking members from across the country.

Speaking from his own experience (David is the "product of the product"), David strives to instill in his members the courage to lead lives unhindered by the expectations of others and driven by purpose. Following in his footsteps, Freedom Founders members attain the tools to become Free for Life™: they can live entirely on the passive income from their real estate investments.

A Recognized Leader in Dentistry and Real Estate

David has been featured in Advantage Forbes Books, The Profitable Dentist, Dental Success Today, The Progressive Orthodontist, MarketWatch, Business Insider, Markets Insider, Value Investing News,

Morningstar, Yahoo! Finance, and *Entrepreneur* magazine, among others. He has been awarded the GKIC Marketer of the Year (2011) award.

He regularly keynotes and presents at live events and has co-hosted multiple virtual and webinar conferences. He is frequently asked to guest present at niche industry mastermind meetings.

David regularly collaborates with countless industry leaders including Dr. Dustin Burleson, Dr. David Maloley, Dr. Michael Abernathy, Dan Sullivan, Steven J. Anderson, Scott Manning, Alastair Macdonald, Dr. Scott Leune, Jason Medley, Shaun McCloskey, Eddie Speed, Daniel Marcos, Christopher Ryan, Dr. John Meis, Dr. Christopher Phelps, and countless others.

At his own events, he has shared the stage with Garrett Gunderson, Chuck Blakeman, Adam Witty, Dr. Dustin Burleson, Dr. David Moffet, Dr. David Maloley, Mike Michalowicz, Tony Rubleski, Jim Palmer, Thomas Blackwell, and many others.

An Expert in the World of Real Estate

David's expertise in the world of real estate includes everything from multi-family apartments, self-storage, commercial properties, mobile home parks, retail properties, single-family rentals, structured notes, private debt, managed funds, and more. He has successfully weathered multiple market corrections—notably using the 2006–2008 downturn to successfully more than double his net worth.

He is regularly consulted in the creation, structure, and economics of large multi-investor syndications, funds, and private investments secured by real estate assets.

RESOURCES

Whenever you're ready, here are additional ways I can help fast-track you to your journey to freedom of time, money, relationships, health, and purpose.

1. **Hear more from me through books, podcast, and blogs**

   - *From High Income to High Net Worth: Alternative Investment Strategies to Stop Trading Time for Dollars and Start Creating True Freedom* by Dr. David Phelps, **www.HighIncomeBook.com**

   - *What's Your Next?: The Blueprint For Creating Your Freedom Lifestyle* by Dr. David Phelps, **www.FindYourNext.com**

   - *Own Your Freedom: Sustainable Wealth for a Volatile World*, with Dan S. Kennedy, **www.OwnYourFreedomBook.com**

   - *The Apprentice Model: A Young Leader's Guide to an Anti-Traditional Life* by Dr. David Phelps, **www.ApprenticeModelBook.com**

   - *The Dentist Freedom Blueprint* podcast, **www.DentistFreedomBlueprint.com**

   - Quick-hitting videos and articles for those looking to jump-start their freedom journey. Visit **www.FreedomFounders.com/Blog**

2. **Schedule a call with me**

   If you'd like to replace your active income with passive investment income within two to three years, and you have at least $1 million in available capital (can include residential or practice equity and business equity), then go to the following link to schedule a call with my team. If it looks like there is a mutual fit, you'll have an opportunity to schedule a call with me directly: **www.FreedomFounders.com/Schedule**

3. **Get your free Retirement Scorecard**

   Benchmark your retirement and wealth-building against hundreds of other practice professionals and business owners. Get personalized feedback on your biggest opportunities and leverage points. Go to **www.FreedomFounders.com/Scorecard** to take the three-minute assessment and get your scorecard.

4. **Receive My Monthly Newsletter: Path to Freedom**

   Get "inside access" to the strategies used by hundreds of dentists, doctors, and practice professionals to create a combined *millions of dollars of passive income*. This publication is packed with strategies, principles, and techniques. It's an easy 30-minute read that will expand your mind and unlock wealth-building potential to catapult you from high income to high net worth. Mailed every month it's a power-packed resource. **www.PathToFreedomNewsletter.com**

5. **Apply to visit the Freedom Founders Community**

   If you'd like to join dozens of dentists, doctors, and practice professionals on the fast track to freedom (two to four years or less), visit **www.FreedomFounders.com/Step-1** to apply for a guest seat.

6. **Work with me directly**

   If you'd like to work directly with me and a small group of my closest investment colleagues, with direct access to the deal-makers and asset classes that I invest in, message me at **admin@FreedomFounders.com** and put "Fast Access" in the subject line, or call (972) 203-6960 (ext. 160) and leave a brief message. Let us know you're interested in the Fast Access program—we'll set up a time with you to talk, find out about your goals, and see if there's a fit.

7. **Access special bonus items at:**
   www.InflationBookResources.com

CLAIM YOUR FREE GIFT FROM DAVID

A Package Containing Case Studies of Professionals Who Are Replacing Their Practice Income with Passive Cash Flow.

You'll receive a book, DVD, and Special Report that share the stories of how real-life dentists "beat the system" and took control of their retirement!

In This Package You Will Discover:

⭐ Stories of actual practitioners who are **shaving decades off of their retirement timeline.**

⭐ Why the "4% rule" and traditional retirement planning is FAILING—and what to do instead.

⭐ The difference between cash flow vs. accumulation.

⭐ How to control real estate without the ownership headaches.

I was ready to exit my practice, David helped me clarify that process.

DR. RON BARNETT

This just gives me a lot of confidence that there is life after dentistry.

DR. MIKE ATENCIO

It would have taken me 7–8 years to get where I've come in just 4 months.

DR. GREG LINNEY

To Request Your Free Case Study Package, Go to:
www.FreeGiftFromDavid.com

GLOSSARY

Bank Reserves. Cash held by banks to meet demands from depositors. Some reserves are held in a vault; however, most are held by the twelve regional Federal Reserve banks. The Federal Reserve sets the reserve requirements based on market conditions and their desire to inflate or decrease the amount of money in circulation.

Central Bank. A bank created by the national government in a country to oversee the nation's financial system and to implement monetary policy. The Federal Reserve is the central bank of the United States, while the Bank of England, Bank of Japan, and the European Central Bank are central banks of their respective nations or unions.

Chained CPI. An index that was developed, much like the CPI, to track inflation in a basket of goods. The index takes into account the substitution of goods and services that consumers might make to allow their dollars to go further. For example, if households normally purchase chicken but the price of chicken increases to such a point the consumers might substitute beef or fish. This is an example of how the Chained CPI would take into account consumer changes. This index limits inflation as compared to the CPI. For some reporting and COLA adjustments, the government uses Chained CPI which can result in lower COLA adjustments.

Consumer Price Index (CPI). The government's index for measuring inflation. Published monthly, the index reflects the price changes in a market basket of goods and services thought to be a typical basket of urban customers.

Core Inflation. A measure of inflation that *does not* include energy and food prices. Many times these two categories are removed for inflation reporting because, the argument goes, they experience higher volatility and shouldn't represent the whole of inflation reporting.

Cost of Living Adjustment (COLA). An automatic adjustment every year of Social Security payments and other governmental payments, such as those for military and federal workers. Many COLAs are found within government pension plans; however, during the '70s most labor unions included this as a key component of their contracts.

Discount Rate. The interest rate at which commercial banks can borrow from the Federal Reserve. Banks turn over collateral to the Fed (typically government or corporate bonds), and in return, the Fed makes loans based on the collateral to the banks.

Federal Funds Rate. The interest rate on the funds the Federal Reserve lends to member banks. This is a tool the Fed uses to increase the money supply by lowering rates or decreasing supply by raising interest rates.

Fiscal Policy. Fiscal policy is a collective term for the taxing and spending actions of governments. In the United States, the national fiscal policy is determined by the executive and legislative branches of the government.

Full Employment. An economic term to indicate that nearly every working-age person has a job or is simply between jobs or not wanting to work. In the United States, under 4% of unemployment is considered full employment.

Gross Domestic Product (GDP). The total value of all the final goods and services produced in a country. GDP could be viewed as the national income.

Great Inflation. The period from the mid-1960s to the early 1980s when the United States experienced its worst inflation outside of the World Wars. CPI inflation rose from 1% in 1960 to a peak of over nearly 13% in 1979 and 1980.

Monetary Policy. Policies used by central banks (like the Federal Reserve in the U.S.) to stimulate or throttle down the economy by either increasing or decreasing money supply, interest rates, credit conditions, or open market operations.

Money Supply. The measurement of what people use to buy and sell. The money supply was broken into M1 consisting of checking, checking deposits, and traveler checks, and M2 consisting of savings accounts, savings certificates, and money market accounts. Today they are both indicated by the term M2.

Money Velocity: The turnover of money in the economic system. For example, if the money supply was $1 trillion, and GDP $20 trillion, the velocity of money would be 20. Currently, the velocity of money sits at an all-time low.

Open Market Operations. A monetary tool used by the Federal Reserve to increase or decrease the money supply. The Fed buys U.S. Treasury securities or other government securities, keeping interest rates low, and by increasing the supply of money, drives asset prices higher because the money that was invested in those securities purchased by the Fed must go somewhere else. In the years after 2009,

Fed Chairman Bernanke began extensive purchasing of assets that drove asset prices higher and created the Wealth Effect for investors.

PCE Price Index. The preferred index by the Federal Reserve, the PCE is viewed as more accurate than the CPI. The biggest difference is that it includes health care spending by insurance companies and government, whereas the CPI only tracks out-of-pocket health care spending. Another major difference is that housing makes up 42% of the CPI and nearly 23% of the PCE.

Wealth Effect. The economic theory utilized for the first time by Ben Bernanke hypothesizes that by driving asset prices higher (i.e. stock market and real estate prices) during economic downturns, confidence will return to the economy sooner as investors see their investment accounts or assets increase in price. Bernanke believed that flooding the market with money and the purchasing of assets by the Fed would drive the recovery after 2008. For these ideas, he would come to be known as "Helicopter Ben."